Sustainable Projections:

Concepts in Film Festival

Management

Alex Fischer

St Andrews Film Studies
Films Need Festivals, Festivals Need Films
Series Editor: Dina Iordanova

First published in Great Britain in 2013 by
St Andrews Film Studies
99 North Street, St Andrews, KY16 9AD
Scotland, United Kingdom
Publisher: Dina Iordanova

Secure on-line ordering:
www.stafs.org

This book is part of the Films Need Festivals, Festivals Need Films Series, edited by
Dina Iordanova.

British Library Cataloguing-in-Publication Data
A catalogue record for this book is available from the British Library.

ISBN 978-0-9563730-8-3 (paperback)

The book is published with the assistance of the Royal Society
of Edinburg and the Centre for Film Studies at the University
of St Andrews.

St Andrews Film Studies promotes greater understanding of,
and access to, international cinema and film culture worldwide.

The University of St Andrews is a charity registered in Scotland,
No. SC013532

University of
St Andrews

Cover design: Izumi Ichyama, Izumi Design

Pre-press: University of St Andrews Print & Design.

Printed in Great Britain by Lightning Source.

Table of Contents

Acknowledgements

I am grateful to Dina Iordanova for her support of both this book and my research. I am similarly grateful to Bruce Molloy for his valued supervisory assistance throughout my PhD. I am indebted to the Leverhulme Trust whose funding of the Dynamics of World Cinema project enabled the revision of my thesis into this book and I thank the reviewers of the manuscript, who provided valuable and considered input and recommendations.

Thanks also to graphic artists Izumi Ichyama and Nick Tran Van Vinn whose skills helped bring to life my ideas and to Stefanie Van de Peer for her assistance with the publication process. To Steve Blackey, whose skills as an editor and textual enhancer proved invaluable. Rock on!

Finally to my family – Mom, Dad, A.J, Lisa and Grandma.

Figures and Charts

List of Abbreviations

BIFFF – Belgium International Fantastic Film Festival

CAFFE – Coordinating Anthropological Film Festivals of Europe

CIFEJ – Centre International du Film pour l'Enfance et la Jeunesse / International Centre of Film for Children and Young People

ECFF – European Co-ordination of Film Festival

EFFFF – European Fantastic Film Festivals Federation

FIAPF – Fédération Internationale des Associations de Producteurs de Films / International Federation of Film Producers Associations

FICC – Fédération Internationale des Ciné-Clubs / International Federation of Film Societies

FIPRESCI – Fédération Internationale de la Presse Cinématographique / The International Federation of Film Critics

IFFS – International Film Festival Summit

NETPAC – Network for the Promotion of Asian Cinema

OSP – Open System Paradigm

OST – Open System Theory

UFFO – Universal Film and Festival Organization

Foreword

The twenty-first century's barometer of all things of consequence, Google, lists over 160 million references to the term 'film festival'. While Google may not represent the most scientific of methods for launching an investigation into the subject, it does demonstrate the degree to which these events have become part of the lifeblood of contemporary film culture. Indeed, the search engine provides a unique glimpse on the film festival landscape in the way that it aligns towering events such as the Cannes International Film Festival (www.festival-cannes.com) right next to niche festivals like the UK-based Minghella Film Festival (www. minghellafilmfestival.com/index.html). Perhaps such an ordering is mere happenstance or is some algorithmically-considered outcome of the Googlebot web-crawling programme, but whatever the reason, the world of film festivals is obviously inhabited by events of all shapes, sizes, geographic locations and themes.

Interestingly, Google also resembles a graveyard for film festivals. Searches for events such as the Czech Republic-based Prague International Film Festival, India-based Cochin International Film Festival or the America-based Taos Talking Pictures Film Festival in New Mexico, unveil the blogs, websites and film programmes of once-vibrant, but now defunct gatherings. And these three festivals are only the tip of the iceberg when it comes to failed events, confirming, if that were required, that there is more to organising a film festival than simply screening films.

Indeed, the threat of failure has spawned a new line of work for consultants who specialise in film festival management. There is, for example, the International Film Festival Summit (IFFS), whose self-proclaimed mission is to 'promote and strengthen the global film festival industry through education, networking, dissemination of information, and the cultivation of high standards for the industry' (IFFS 2009). The IFFS offers what it terms a Certified Film Festival Professional Program: a two-day course that optimistically claims to provide 'an in-depth training curriculum covering the most important elements involved in film festival work' (Box Office Network 2009). Similarly, there are a number of film festival-focussed self-help resources ranging from on-line, step-by-step guides such as those presented by *eHow* (How to Organize a Film Festival 2008) and ideastap.com (Humphreys 2011), to more comprehensive instructional sources produced by distinguished organisations, like the One World Human Rights Film Festival (Porybna 2009) and the British Film Institute (Eldridge and Voss 2010).

Regardless of instruction or specialised training, it is difficult for any one person to guarantee the successful management of any event. It takes more to facilitate the functional needs of a film festival than simply attending a two-day programme or merely having strong film industry contacts and connections. In fact, so unique and unforeseeable are the challenges of operation that film festival consultant Lauri Tanner wastes no time in declaring that 'no liability is assumed for incidental or consequential damages in connection with or arising out of the use of the information or programs contained' (Tanner 2009: 2).

Successful film festival management is entirely based on the skilful manoeuvring of an event through a host of socially contrived conditions that, due to their circumstantial nature, have never appeared before and will likely never appear in the same form again. With this in mind, film festival organisers should have a healthy scepticism of any one-size-fits all notions of 'the best' way to run an event. Such a panacea for the trials of film festival operation simply does not exist. In fact, so multifaceted and challenging are the situations faced by film festival organisers, that for the director of the Vancouver International Film Festival (www.viff.org), Alan Franey, even the mere discussion of their management can be as 'discouraging as it is encouraging' (Tanner 2009: 7).

It was this very idea of film festival operation representing something so convoluted and multidimensional that a concrete explanation of it was deemed too difficult, that posed the impetus for my PhD thesis (*Conceptualising Basic Film Festival Operation: an Open System Paradigm*) upon which this monograph is based. The goal of my research is to identify and, effectively, to map the basic operational structure of film festivals and the means by which these events either succeed or fail. A decade of research into the subject was conducted and the methods employed included both an in-depth study of film festival literature, that is, publications produced by or about events, as well as personal interviews with film festival practitioners such as festival directors, distributors, funding agencies and film board members.

Initially, writing about the complexities of film festival operation proved to be just as discouraging for me as their discussion was for Alan Franey. The results of the research indicated that the majority of managerial obstacles faced by film festival organisers were almost always connected to social aspects of festival operation. So, while many film festival organisers shared similar experiences, each particular situation was unique in itself. It was only when I began to analyse information through an Open System Paradigm that the challenges inherent to film festival operation such as filmmaker participation, funding body satisfaction, and distributor interest, began to make sense.

The Open System Paradigm is a managerial philosophy that supports strategic decision-making while remaining flexible to the ever-changing conditions inherent to the film festival environment. This philosophy is expanded in chapter two an illustrated further throughout this book.

This book is not intended to be a 'how to' guide or a DIY manual, but rather a resource that strives to present film festival operation in a manner that makes it clear, concise and understandable, and in a way that can contribute to an event's sustainability.

There are two concepts that require explanation before we proceed any further. First, the phrase 'film festival operation' as it is used here, is an overarching concept intended to represent those steps that are essential to facilitate a film festival but does not seek to indicate the day-to-day tasks that form part of these actions. So when it is said that film festival operation is a complex web of social connectivity, readers should imagine the big picture indicative of participant interaction as opposed to minor details such as phone calls, emails or other means of communication that are the more personal tools of this social connectedness. This book will not tell you who to talk to or what to say, but it will tell you what you are actually doing when you do make those calls.

With the phrase 'film festival environment', I refer to the external forces (political, cultural, etc.) that are likely to influence operational capabilities. Not unlike a natural ecosystem, there are certain participants and infrastructure-based needs that must be in place in order for an event to function viably. Volatility is characteristic of the film festival environment and therefore successful film festival management requires an organiser to be completely attuned to any potential changes that may upset the regular operation of the event.

Running a film festival is a nearly masochistic undertaking that leaves anyone who attempts it open to the vagaries of time, money and space (and other people) in a way that serves to define the inherent chaos in any socially-constructed activity. But that does not mean it cannot be done. In the chapters that follow, readers will encounter various conceptual lenses through which to view a number of the factors that influence successful film festival management. The first chapter will discuss the social connectivity of film festivals. Paramount in this chapter is the concept of a collective identity and the influence that participants such as filmmakers, distributors and sponsors have on the functional abilities of an event. The second chapter identifies film festival operation as an Open System. The information presented here constructs a simple yet robust route to the understanding of the basic operational procedures required to keep a film festival viable. The third chapter contemplates successful film festival operation and proposes eight strategies that are

Alex Fischer

recognised to increase the Open System capabilities of an event. The fourth chapter comprises a narrative case study of the Australian-based Gold Coast Film Fantastic (www.gcfilmfestival.com/) and details the action taken by organisers (of whom the author was one) to give new life to and re-energise a defunct event. The short conclusion examines the motivations behind the discontinuance of one of Eastern Europe's oldest film festivals, Latvia's International Film Festival Arsenal (www.arsenals. lv/), in light of the Open System elements noted previously.

It is my sincere hope that the examples and the case study that inform the concepts presented in the following pages, will assist potential and existing festival organisers to better comprehend what is required in order to achieve sustainable film festival operation. The purpose of this book then is to offer festival organisers this understanding of sustainability for film festivals, so that they will be more capable of explaining their motivations to those external to the intricacies of the event.

Chapter 1
Bound and Gagged:
Social Connectivity and Film Festivals

A stuffy, windowless room. A large, rectangular table. Around this table sit nine people; five are in business suits, the others sport a more casual look. They are the film festival board and they are staring intensely at you, the festival director. Opening Night is three months away and this is the monthly meeting at which the progress of the event is outlined, concerns are raised and, most importantly, decisions are made. You begin your report: 'It's complicated...'

Flashback to two months ago. An internationally-recognised visual artist has accepted an invitation to participate in the film festival. The project includes a multimedia, performance-based piece in which live music, dancers and video projection will be married to form what, for marketing purposes, has been labelled 'Expanded Cinema'. During the next eight weeks there is overwhelming support from the board for this ambitious project and all of the puzzle pieces seem to be fitting neatly into place. The acclaimed artist's reputation means that funding has been relatively easy to secure. A number of local musicians and dance troupes have eagerly volunteered their services just to be a part of this once-in-a-lifetime event and, at last, key politicians have taken notice, pledging their attendance and hailing the artistic and cultural sensibility of the festival.

Then things get complicated. Flash forward to two nights before the board meeting. You are Skyping with the artist. Despite being located on opposite sides of the world, communication has been excellent and this digital *rendez-vous* promises to be short and sweet; it's only an update of the project's progress. You explain that the venue has been secured, lighting and staging companies contracted, and that publicity in local schools has commenced. By all accounts it has been smooth sailing and it seems there will be very little trouble in achieving the artist's vision. When asked about the dancers you say that the local troupe will be e-mailing their ideas regarding choreography within the week and that the eager musicians have nearly completed the soundtrack. In short, everything is going to work out fine, just fine. Fine, that is, until the artist suddenly explains that it will be necessary to tweak the concept. 'How big a tweak are we talking?' you ask with trepidation. 'Well,' the artist begins, staring intensely into the camera's lens. 'I believe it is important that the work explores the nation's history honestly. So, the actors will be covered in thick black body paint while dancers bound in chains trudge laboriously across the stage under dark blue lighting giving the necessary oppressively gloomy atmosphere representative of the horror of the colonisation of Australia.'

There is a pregnant pause as a line between the artistic process and creative contempt is drawn in Skype's virtual sand. Desperately trying to avoid offending the artist, you caution that the slow wheels of bureaucracy may prevent any drastic conceptual changes, fumblingly explaining and attempting excuses: 'The idea is interesting but such a major deviation from the accepted project would require the board's approval and the funding agencies would need to be contacted to see if such an alteration is permissible, and then there's the occupational health and safety issue regarding the chains and…' – you fade into silence… a long silence… until – 'there is also the chance that the board and the funders may not wish to support a project that focuses on such a sensitive issue in such a confronting manner'.

After a brief tirade, during which a conscious stream of invective thought unleashes rapid fire observations at you about 'my art', 'inferior festival', 'cultural wasteland' and 'unprofessional charlatans', the artist suddenly leans close to the computer screen, eyeballing you through the ether, and yells into the surprisingly sensitive pinhole microphone 'What are YOU going to do about it?'.

What I just described is an aspect of film festival leadership that is difficult to grasp for those on the outside of the intricacies of operation. Whether it is a filmmaker complaining about unbalanced sound at a screening, sponsors upset at the choice of the wine on Opening Night, or a movie star not satisfied with the size of his hotel suite, you must be very aware of the battles raging around and within the festival, aware of that moment when the solution calls for a compromise or for digging-in and defending the event.

The answer is not always clear and each situation is likely to be interpreted differently depending on the experience of, information available to, and possible consequences recognised by, the decision makers. The artist's question 'What are YOU going to do about it?' is loaded because of the fact that the answer ultimately rests on how other participants involved in the project will (or may) react to this particular tweak.

In my role as a festival organiser I have observed that those outside of direct film festival management (like board members, patrons and even volunteer staff), while they may have an idea as to how their particular film festival functions, they also have a tendency to

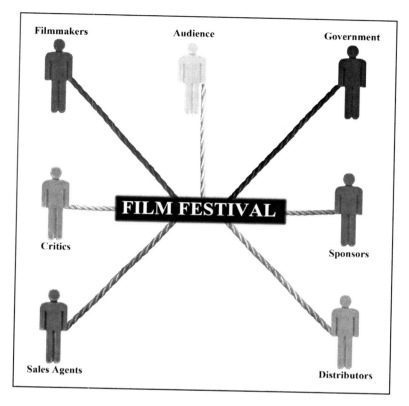

Fig. 1: Simplified film festival interaction. Image by A. Fischer.

oversimplify the social connections that ultimately tie an event together. Their generalised view of film festival operation sees resources such as films and funding being acquired through consistent and designated channels, and special guests and the human resources they represent recruited via more specialised means, such as through personal contacts. These elements are then all brought together at a designated time. Simple.

While such an understanding is not entirely incorrect, it is simplistic, and it can lead to picturing the film festival operation as merely a series of isolated exchanges. That is, as multiple, serial one-on-one relationships between the film festival and each of its many participants, as visualised in Fig. 1.

Here, a hypothetical film festival is served by seven external participant groups. The connection between the film festival and each individual group is formed by a shared benefit or need. On the one hand, filmmakers may use a film festival as a platform to showcase their work, while government agencies may provide funding as a means of achieving their mandate. The film festival, on the other hand, receives vital resources that it requires for operation, in the form of films, money or attendance. In this symbolic symbiotic representation everyone wins; if the relationship does not work out, the connection is simply severed.

Such a diagram makes participation in a festival based on a finite number of connections apparently easy to understand, but for those with experience of managing a film festival something as seemingly simple as the withdrawal of even a single participant from the event presents a complex situation. The social connectivity that underlies a film festival is better represented as a complex web of networks. In the diagram in Fig. 2, each participant is seen to be not only connected with the film festival but also with others who are taking part in the event. This adds further layers of complexity to the scenario. Should a filmmaker now decide to withdraw, then it is possible that the appeal of the film festival could be compromised and that consequently, audience members and/or critics may decide not to participate or attend at all. The outcome of any withdrawal can, therefore, be seen to influence not only the film festival's ability to operate but also the incentive that drives others to participate.

The social connectivity of film festival operation is obvious when it has been pointed out. Film festival expert Dina Iordanova puts the case plainly and simply when she states that 'festivals need films' (2009: 25); the acquisition of films requires that festival organisers interact with an environment external to their event by building relationships with film sources, e.g. distributors and filmmakers. According to sociologist Talcott Parsons, such interactions are driven by the 'optimization of gratification' (1951: 5) of both parties' needs.

Optimisation of gratification fundamentally works because, as Iordanova also declares, 'films need festivals' (2009: 24). The interaction between film festivals and film suppliers appears mutually beneficial. The term 'appears' is used deliberately here, because, as the diagram demonstrates (Fig. 2), the relationships between film festivals and their external participants are rarely simple one- or even two-way affairs. However, it is enough here to declare that the social connectivity between a film festival and its participants is based on motivated participation with the intention of facilitating/creating a beneficial outcome. Sounds nice and friendly, but in reality, everyone is in it for themselves.

Those individuals and groups that participate in film festivals and ultimately contribute to their operation are topics of frequent discussion. Film festival insider Mark Peranson lists seven 'interest groups' (2009: 31)

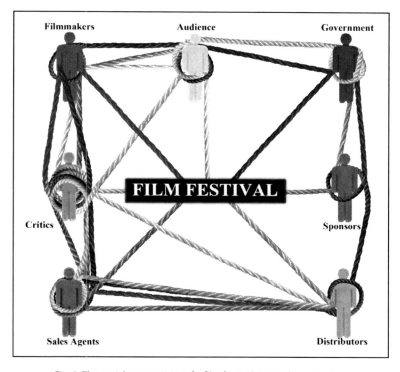

Fig. 2: The social connectivity of a film festival. Image by A. Fischer.

that attend film festivals. He also distinguishes between the reasons for their participation in festivals. These groups are differentiated according to the various needs each has for a film festival, and indeed festivals themselves are delineated by Peranson according to a particular corresponding classificatory system. So, for example, a sales agent utilises a 'business festival' to promote and sell films, but would use an 'audience festival' primarily as a means of generating money from hire fees (Ibid.).

A similar means of categorisation is presented in SECOR Consulting's analysis of Canadian film festivals. Their report identifies 'three main types of stakeholders: general public, film professionals and public partners' (2004: 3). The rationale behind this categorisation is to draw attention to the various expectations of different participants and to set a standard in terms of the quality of the performance expected from the respective festivals.

The phenomenal influx of people who attend film festivals has also been the subject of much attention. Film critic Kenneth Turan notes that attendance at Sundance increased by almost 900 per cent between 1985 and 1999 (2002: 32). During the early 1990s, film festival commentators Cari Beauchamp and Henri Béhar were describing the flow of people into Cannes as

> thirty thousand people from throughout the world [who] converge for that fortnight to see and be seen, buy and be bought, sell and be sold, review and be reviewed, promote and be promoted, and/or somehow be a part of the movies. (1992: 21)

The fact that film festivals require socially-based participation should not be viewed as merely a by-product of their functionality, but instead, as a critical, indeed intrinsic requirement of their actual operation. This characteristic contributes to their importance as 'sites of passage' (de Valck 2007: 36) and confirms the notion that the appropriate film festival management sees film festival organisers constructing a social web that strengthens operation.

Other factors can complicate managerial decisions even further: film festival operation often progresses from a chaotic state to near paralysis. This chaotic state is created by the environment and is the result of an interplay of factors that range from changes in cinematic trends to business-related phenomena, like the rise and fall of currency rates, political unrest, or biological epidemics and natural disasters. Veteran film critic Todd McCarthy explains that the Cannes International Film Festival has historically been threatened by such chaotic events as 'enormous upheavals in the global film industry, changing tastes, political disruptions, artistic controversies and the challenges of countless other younger festivals around the world' (1997: 11). Similarly, film festival researcher Pauline Webber reports of Australia's Sydney Film Festival (www.sff.org.au) that it

> had to reposition itself, philosophically and practically, to deal with the more challenging production environment created by the conflicting demands of audience, filmmakers, funding agencies and the many other groups with investment in Australian film culture. (2005: Chapter 3)

The dynamic nature of the film festival environment requires film festival management to be an on-going process involving the expectation, manipulation and utilisation of frequent environmental changes in order to attract and retain participants. For example, Webber explains that if the Sydney Film Festival were 'to survive long term it would need to move with the times' (2005: Chapter 2). Similarly, McCarthy comments that sudden environmental changes that 'could have marked the end of Cannes instead provoked it to reform' (1997: 15).

Paralysis, however, results from the binding nature of decisions and commitments that ultimately dictate a film festival's final structure. An artistic decision to feature a Pier Paolo Pasolini retrospective calls for a narrowing of focus in order to bring this aspect of the festival programme to the forefront and to fruition. It also dictates the details according to which distributors must be contacted, which potential censorship issues must be addressed, and how the most appreciative audience may be attracted.

Paralysis can also be indicative of the loss of creative or organisational control that can occur when entities from outside of the operational structure of the film festival itself become entrenched in the decision-making process. This is interference. The dependency f a film festival on a major sponsor will undoubtedly influence how the festival organisers operate the event with regard to the needs and expectations of that particular benefactor. This relationship may prevent organisers from making certain structural changes for fear of potentially jeopardising established support. In 1973 for example, the Benson and Hedges Tobacco Company cancelled its sponsorship of a short film competition facilitated by the Sydney Film Festival because the content of one of the submissions 'was found not to be consonant with the image the company wished to project' (Hope 2004: 194).

Then there is the fact that film festivals require various particular types of participants, each supplying diverse but essential resources. This can contribute to paradoxical situations in which the gratification of one participant becomes grounds for the withdrawal of another. Such conflict sees film festival organisers grappling with the challenges associated with collective identity, the process whereby participants invest their personal ideas and values into an organisation and come to view themselves, through this contribution, as being integral to the event and as collaborating in its success. Film festivals, however, typically have various participants, each with their own contributions (and agendas), who struggle and come into conflict to shape the identity of the event according to their own designs. Therefore, contributions such as these, while obviously important, can be the source of many difficulties for the festival organiser and have the potential to undermine an event, preventing it from reaching its full potential. Organisational theorists Jeffrey Pfeffer and Gerald Salancik note that while it is 'clearly easier to satisfy a single criterion, or a mutually compatible set of criteria', the difficulties associated with the 'conflicting' and competing demands posed by 'a variety of participants' makes the management of organisations complex and challenging, since only very rarely does an all-accommodating solution exist (2003: 261).

In 2009, the Melbourne International Film Festival (MIFF) (miff.com. au) made global headlines when British filmmaker Ken Loach threatened to withdraw his film *Looking for Eric* (UK, France, Italy, Belgium, Spain, 2009) from the event if the organisers accepted funding from the Israeli Government to host Tatia Roenthal, director of the Israeli/Australian co-production *$9.99* (2009). The Canadian Broadcasting Corporation reported, 'Loach wrote to festival director Richard Moore, saying he was not protesting Israeli films or filmmakers, but objected to Israel's "illegal occupation of Palestinian land, destruction of homes and livelihoods"' (2009). Moore did not capitulate and even went so far as to call Loach's request 'blackmail' (Canadian Broadcasting Corporation 2009). Political intricacies apart, this reaction illustrates the organisers' unswerving stance and demonstrates the strength of resolve to retain control over the situation. It ultimately preserved the legitimacy of the film festival and prevented a precedent under which participants could set, at the expense of others, their own conditions for future involvement. Loach's film was indeed withdrawn – certainly a loss, but the strength and integrity displayed by the organisers was undoubtedly gratifying to others involved with the festival.

Compare this situation with that of the Edinburgh International Film Festival (www.edfilmfest.org.uk). Also in 2009, the Scottish film festival was challenged by Ken Loach to reject funding from the Israeli Embassy in London, because the 'massacres and state terrorism in Gaza make this money unacceptable' (Haaretz Service 2009). However, unlike MIFF, the organisers of the Edinburgh event relented under the pressure of a possible boycott and returned the £300 (US$475) grant money meant to cover the travel expenses of Israeli filmmaker Tali Shalom Eze. Though the film festival still paid to have the filmmaker attend, irreparable damage to the event's reputation had been done. Instead of resolving the conflict, the capitulation led to further criticism: Sir Jeremy Isaacs, the founding chief of Channel Four, one of the UK's main television channels, called into question the organisers' decision to 'allow someone who has no real position, no rock to stand on, to interfere with their programming' (Haaretz Service 2009).

Let us return briefly to the situation with the artist described at the opening of this chapter: 'What are you going to do about it'? Some of the best advice I have been given with regards to the type of relationship a film festival director must have with print handlers, distributors, filmmakers and artists, was imparted to me by Michael Selwyn, the managing director of Paramount Pictures Australia. A festival director, he reasoned, 'must be part bully and part whore' (Selwyn 2006). Of course one must not take this observation too literally (festival participation would become extremely interesting in that case), but the clear and correct implication is that film festival organisers must stand up for what they want, or adopt a more conciliatory and obliging attitude, as required.

Managing a film festival requires adopting a particular mind-set, one that is both attentive to the present, yet also aware of the implications that certain actions are likely to have on future events. Understanding how the interconnectivity of participation can influence operation is a skill acquired with experience. The crucial lesson is that no single participant is worth endangering the festival for – unless the event is known or wishes to become known for controversy. At all costs, avoid damaging the reputation of the event, as such damage is difficult to repair.

The key concept to keep in mind when negotiating the minefield of participation is that for every hard and fast rule there is an equally viable contingency that contradicts it. This is the nature of chaos. Conquering this situation is not easy and while some may be reluctant to identify film festival directors who successfully navigate this hazardous terrain as gifted, it is undeniable that they do possess a certain ability to read and to react to situations with uncommon skill and comprehension. It is my belief that such awareness cannot be taught and, like an elite athlete or talented musician, it is simply a part of their being. Yet not all is lost; the following chapter aims to piece together the fundamental aspects of film festival operation in such a way that will open up avenues towards a more innovative and insightful comprehension of the subject.

Chapter 2

Open for Business:
The System Behind
Film Festival Operation

It is astounding how much information is produced by and about film festivals each year. Press releases, festival reports, event recaps, programming notes, posters, on-line advertising, web articles, submission forms, acquittals, invoices; the list is endless. And then there are the lists themselves, and the spread sheets and databases, all produced week in, week out, year round by festivals and their participants. Too much information to ever be synthesised into a fully operational understanding of any of these events. Accomplished film festival director Darryl MacDonald is 'always amazed' when he gets 'a call from someone wanting to start a film festival who thinks that some kind of blueprint exists that will make everything simple' (1998: 40).

Actually, the idea of a blueprint is not so far-fetched. Film festivals are, structurally speaking at least, easy to observe and explain. They are, in essence, 'sites of exhibition' (Iordanova 2009: 26), places where films are collected to be screened on a designated date at a specified time. In fact, the experiential nature of these events means they are actually the obvious place for film festival organisers to look for managerial answers and inspiration.

Film festival directors have successfully adopted the operational structures of other film festivals on numerous occasions in their attempts to facilitate a similar type of event. The organisers of the California-based Mill Valley Film Festival (www.mvff.com) in America, for example, relied on the observations and experiences they encountered at the Telluride Film Festival (www.telluridefilmfestival.org) in Colorado to inform and inspire their own operation (Benson 1998: 149). Similarly, Michael Kutza, founder of the Chicago International Film Festival (www.chicagofilmfestival.com), decided after visiting Cannes in 1962 that he would create 'a similar event' (Klady 1998: 153).

However, because those who attend a film festival see only a fraction of the organisational complexity of the event, merely copying is not likely to offer the best solution when it comes to assessing operational difficulties. It is a situation that generally causes little harm, although the opposite can be true should an attendee decide to start their own film festival and underestimate the amount of co-ordination, negotiation and time and effort required to facilitate a functional event.

The aim of this chapter is to present a basic yet comprehensive conceptual framework of film festival functionality. It is, in essence, a structural outline of film festival operation, purposely designed to highlight those aspects that are imperative for successful and sustainable film festival management. The concepts presented here are not preoccupied with the glitz and glamour that make an event sexy, but rather with the organisational arrangement according to which a film festival is built.

Similar to a connect-the-dots puzzle, the conceptualisation of basic film festival operation is a step-by-step process. It begins with identifying and assessing those organisational dots that are required for operation and the means by which lines may be drawn between them so as to deliver a recognisable picture at the end. With this in mind, certain aspects presented may at times seem laborious, technical or pedantic, but in the same way that skipping a numbered dot on a puzzle may result in the drawing of a distorted picture, so too will not taking the time to make clear the conceptual links, result in an incomplete construction of a robust framework for festival operation.

The first step in forming such a framework begins with the understanding that a film festival is a system, and that a system is an 'assemblage or combination of things or parts forming a complex or unitary whole' (Macquarie 1997: 2150). The systematic operation of a film festival is readily observable, from the assemblage of programming and attendance of festival guests, to the complex combination of components that constitute the unity of the event itself, bookended by an Opening Night and a Closing Night.

Viewing a film festival as a system is a rewarding exercise, not least because it emphasises the consequential nature of decision-making. As mentioned earlier, the participation of filmmakers, funding bodies, distributors and others in a festival are rarely isolated events. Managerial choices regarding the inclusion of individuals or groups must reflect the best possible situation for the event as a unified whole. Presenting a film festival as a system also promotes a logical approach to operation and enables organisers to identify where procedural pitfalls may exist. The inclusion of a film in a festival programme, for example, involves a series of interrelated events and elements that must be taken into consideration before any work is screened. An examination of programming will serve to illustrate this.

Films are commonly selected for programming after having been viewed at another film festival or via screeners issued by distribution companies or sales agents. Alternatively, films can be selected sight-unseen, in which case it is attention in the form of media stories concerning a particular title, or the reputation of an individual involved with the film's production, that motivates the festival organisers to actively pursue it for programming. These films often come to a film festival through official invitation: the communicated acceptance of a title into a festival by a festival staff member that is then mailed electronically or traditionally to the film's source. Films can also be programmed via unsolicited entry, in which case the title is entered into the festival via a designated channel, by, for example, a call for entries. In this case, if the title is selected – which often requires the formation of a selection panel – an official invitation is, once again, communicated to the film's source.

It is at this point that communication between the film festival organiser and the filmmakers, rights holders, distributors, etc. commences. Consecutively, screening fees are negotiated, dates of shipment set, publicity stills requested and various other activities undertaken, such as the title's placement within the programming, attention to technical requirements with regard to the venues, issues of censorship, electronic press kits (EPKs); and all these actions are undertaken virtually simultaneously.

The exhibition of the film involves the cueing of tapes or print preparation, the formatting of aspect ratios, test screenings to ensure screening quality, in addition to the selling of tickets and the accommodation of an audience at a venue to view the film. The screening may also be accompanied by a short introductory speech, in which case the presenter will be required to compose a brief of information, which may include, and is certainly not limited to, outlining the film's production, acknowledging the key individuals involved in that production, providing tips on how to read the film; the list goes on.

But that is not all. Once the screening is over, the film must be returned, which requires the breaking down of the print/repackaging of the tape, more communication with the title's source regarding its next destination (usually another film festival on the circuit), shipping logistics, and finally delivery by courier or some other means of transportation.

Of course, a plethora of other elements is involved, particularly if an unforeseen event disrupts the flow of the process. Yet even this simplistic rendering serves to indicate the number and intricacies of systemic actions and reactions that (could) unfold during this process. Similar examples could be constructed concerning funding or the procuring and hosting of film festival guests, or promoting the event, and on and on, that would further display how film festivals exemplify the characteristics of a system. What becomes apparent is the efficacy of taking a systematic approach to understanding film festival operation by deconstructing the process of the screening of a film into a series of individual actions which, when reassembled correctly, ultimately contribute to the festival's successful functionality.

It is time to begin to examine the concepts that underlie this systematic framework. But to truly gain the strategic benefits of this system-based framework, a more technical, theoretical representation must be constructed. The rationale for involving theory is not to complicate matters, but rather to utilise what science has already articulated to deepen our knowledge of what actually drives film festival operation. That is, by identifying a film festival as a system, festival organisers are able to use scientific thought to logically link action to results.

We must first recognise that, due to the dependency on their environment outlined in the previous chapter, film festivals are in fact a special type of system. This dependency on external factors is a defining characteristic of what is called an Open System. Open System organisations are completely dependent on the participation of external groups and individuals – participants – in order to operate. Without these interactions, and without successful acquisition of an adequate amount of resources from external sources, an Open System organisation fails to function.

Though many film festivals are able to manufacture some of their own resources, e.g. publicity, venues and even, on occasion, films, such production does not match the scale or range of resources a festival requires to become truly self-sufficient. The ultimate understanding of film festival operation recognises its environmental dependency. If a film festival was able to produce its own films, manufacture its own technology and supply its own audience it would, in effect, have zero dependency on its environment.

Significant research has been carried out with regard to the vitality of Open System organisations. Perhaps the best known is the appropriately titled Open System Theory (OST), which forms the structural centrepiece of Daniel Katz and Robert L. Kahn's seminal work *The Social Psychology of Organizations* (1978). The authors are acknowledged leaders among those concerned with the theoretical application of the concept to social-based organisations and they use OST to better their own and our understandings of social systems.

Open System Theory is a conceptual framework of operation. Its strength lies in its generalisability: it is applicable across a range of studies and disciplines. Open System Theory has been employed to 'help understand the challenges (and opportunities) symphony orchestra organizations face' (Roelofs 2008) among many other things. More importantly, Open System Theory has also been used to analyse how non-profit organisations are able to gain competitive advantages through their implementation of what is termed 'strategic alliances' (Starnes 2000: 16). In order for managers to think strategically, they need to 'see the[ir] organisation as a system that functions by acquiring inputs from the environment, transforming them in some way, and discharging outputs back into the environment' (Ibid.). These interactions with the environment are extremely important and have only been touched upon so far.

As discussed in the first chapter, film festivals offer gratification to their participants. Gratification is, of course, to be understood as the benefit that comes from interaction. Depending on who the particular participants are, the gratification that they receive will differ across the festival. So, a distributor will be gratified if, at the end of the festival, the film that they have contributed to the event has screened in sold-out theatres and received glowing reviews in the newspapers. The transformation that Becky Starnes identifies would, in this particular case, consist of the actual screening of the film as well as the creation and forwarding of written copy to the media for distribution. As sites of exhibition, film festivals' primary transformative actions come in the screening of films, which, by being projected, watched and opined about, are transformed into something more than just a movie. They become a 'great movie', a 'thought-provoking film' or, in dire cases, 'celluloid time sinks'. Such an earned reputation (with the exception of the latter poor review, naturally) can then be output into the (media) environment in order to gratify the supplier of the film. So, indeed, films need festivals and festivals need films.

Katz and Kahn acknowledge that although all Open Systems share 'common characteristics by virtue of being open', they may have 'other characteristics' indicative of their individual operation (1978: 23). For example, an automotive factory is obviously an Open System: components must be imported into the factory where they are transformed by the labour force and output as cars. Yet, a film festival represents a unique type of Open System due to its function within the film industry and within society as a whole. That is, because film festivals are first and foremost sites of exhibition they will rarely enter into the physical process of film production in the same way in which an automotive factory manufactures cars. Even in unique cases – such as a 24-hour film festival where filmmakers attempt to shoot and edit a film within that set period of time – festival organisers still primarily occupy the role of the exhibitor, because it is on the screening of the resultant films that the entire event is scheduled and ultimately based.

A consequence of this exhibitor role is that film festival operation differs from other Open Systems in being of noticeably shorter duration. The actual physical processes of operation – multiple screenings, hosting festival guests, bestowing awards – generally occur only once, at a given time and for a set period. This distinctive operational structure sets film festivals apart from many other types of Open System social organisations, which have a year-round existence.

So, as a special class of Open System, organisations have properties that are uniquely their own, yet they also have properties in common with all Open Systems. Katz and Kahn produce a list of 10 characteristics that they say 'define all Open Systems' (1978: 23-30). Not all of these characteristics are necessary for the formulation of a framework for basic film festival operation but are better employed when examining an event understood to be in an advanced stage of operation. For example, certain Open System characteristics prove invaluable when assessing situations such as recruitment beyond established audience groups or interpreting feedback gathered through proven operation, but are of little consequence if those aspects essential to film festival operation are not implement first. Things will be considerably more productive if only the first five are recognised as being critical here to representing basic functionality:

1. Importation of energy

2. The throughput [i.e. transformation] of energy

3. The output of energy

4. Re-energisation: systems as cycles of events

5. Negative entropy

This modified application will be referred to as an Open System Paradigm (OSP) so as not to confuse the concepts and ideas proposed here with those original to OST. It is important to note that the proposed OSP should be seen as descriptive rather than prescriptive. That is, the framework does not address specific aspects of individual operation, e.g. it does not attempt to explain what intricate and detailed measures film festival organisers must undertake to solicit film entries for their programming. However, it does serve as a means to identify those processes that drive functionality. It is a framework that reveals what is happening.

The application of the Open System Paradigm framework views basic film festival operation as a logical linear progression. That is, there is a certain order to follow and number two cannot precede number one: the throughput of energy cannot take place prior to the importation of energy. Such a progression promotes a systematic examination of film festival operation and one only needs to follow the flow of resources, to connect the dots from input to output, in order to formulate an understanding of how any particular film festival is utilising the resources which it is importing from its participants. The following diagram illustrates this operational chain of events (Fig. 3). Each characteristic is identified as a phase. The fifth characteristic, negative entropy, will not necessarily be identified as the fifth phase but as constantly present factor. The term 'negative' is misleading because the process is actually positive. It is an involved concept represented by the arrows at the centre of the illustration. It therefore requires more attention regarding how it should be perceived in film festival operation. Its incorporation, along with the notion of the cyclical nature of Open Systems, indicates the impetus underlying the progression of festival operations, and the logic of doing this will become apparent as the discussion moves along.

With this notion of a linear progression in mind, film festival operation can be understood to commence with the importation of resources. Identifying resource importation – input – as phase 1 of festival operation underlines its primacy within the operational scheme. If a film festival is not able to obtain any resource input then it is physically and logically unable to operate. It is for this reason that the input of resources is identified as the single most important aspect of film festival operation. It cannot be stressed highly enough that without the adequate importation of resources to form the basis from which the remaining phases may be brought to bear, the ability of a film festival to function is fatally compromised and its failure imminent.

This is not to devalue the remaining phases, however. On the contrary, the input of resources alone cannot guarantee that an adequate system of interaction will occur, nor is it enough, in isolation, to sustain film festival operation. Rather, as resources advance into throughput and output (phases 2 and 3 respectively), film festival organisers must ensure that the resources are utilised in accordance with the conditions under which they were first secured, i.e. a film festival organiser must transform and output those elements that will deliver a participant's gratification. Because the screening of a single film does not constitute a festival, participants' gratification is crucial as it serves to encourage further participation in the quest for more gratification, and that means more films (or other resources). This occurs during phase 4 and is represented

Alex Fischer

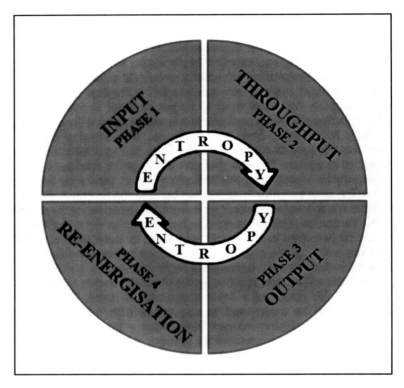

Fig. 3: The Open System Paradigm (OSP). Image by A. Fischer.

on the diagram as re-energisation: the environment is primed, as it were, by successful outputting, to continue the process again at phase 1. Should a film festival organiser successfully secure a film for exhibition, but fail to transform and output the film in a manner that satisfies the initial motivation for the film supplier's participation (the credits were cut during the screening and the film's title was misspelled in the press release), then re-energisation is unlikely and the consequences are dire.

Such a failure could result in reduced motivation for future participation, a toughening of standards governing continued or future interaction; extra, possibly restrictive, control over the throughput and output processes; or the severing of ties completely. Alternatively, should the transformation and output of a resource match or exceed the resource provider's expectations, then it is likely that the next cycle of input would see an increase in their level of participation. Film festival organisers who are able to show that they can, for example, successfully manage government funding, may find themselves eligible for larger grants, thus increasing the potential for input from that particular source (Highsted 2009: 40).

The characteristics of each of these phases, including their points of commencement and conclusion, will bear further detailed discussion.

Input – Phase 1

This first phase sees the securing of a resource from the environment. By securing I mean that the resource comes under the control of the film festival organiser. Such control can be identified as the depositing of money into a bank account, the receiving of a film by the print handler or even the arrival of a guest at the film festival. It is important to note that until the resource is under the management of the film festival organisers, it cannot be considered to be a guaranteed input. As much as one would wish, promises, legal contracts, business deals and handshakes do not constitute guarantees; circumstances may change that can keep a promised resource from entering into the film festival regardless of the assurances made for its potential importation. The unexpected arrest and subsequent detention of film director Roman Polanski by Swiss authorities while he was en route to the 2009 Zurich Film Festival (zff.com/en/home/), is just one example of the uncertainty endemic to resource importation. Needless to say, the unanticipated incarceration of this high-profile guest left the festival organiser 'shocked and unable to comprehend this situation' (Macnab 2009).

Tim Highsted, of both the London International Film Festival (www.bfi.org.uk/lff/) and San Francisco International Film Festival (festival.sffs.org), provides a cautionary tale of attempting to secure a physical film print from its source just seven days prior to its scheduled screening at a festival; having to deal with customs issues, with the print's quality and with the potential for the film itself to have sustained damage, can take time to overcome and must be considered by the organisers (Tanner 2009: 46). Charles Masters, European features editor for the *Hollywood Reporter*, even gives two accounts of secured films effectively being 'stolen' by other film festivals at the eleventh hour before physical operation began (2004). It is for this reason that this phase is identified as beginning with control of the resource being given to the film festival organisers, thus effectively reducing the likelihood of such theft or resource withdrawal.

The importation of a resource can only be said to have concluded when that particular resource begins its transformation, in the second phase of operation. The point at which this phase takes place can be difficult to ascertain, since different resources may be incorporated into

Alex Fischer

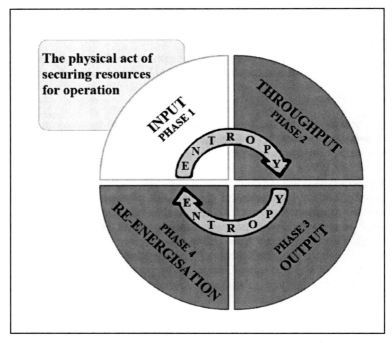

Fig. 4: Input – the first phase of the Open System Paradigm. Image by A. Fischer.

an operation in a multitude of ways. The defining feature of crossing this so-called input-transformation barrier is, in most cases, a change in the physical properties of the resource. For example, funding allocated to a film festival can be transformed by being transferred into a distributor's bank account to pay the hire fees of a film. The act of transferring the funding changes the physical properties of the original resource so that currency has, in effect, become a film.

Throughput / transformation – Phase 2

Transformation commences when a resource is manipulated by organisers in order to perform a specific role or task. The transformation of some resources is less obvious, especially when money or physical evidence, such as a film, is not involved. The selection of films for programming is a form of transformation. As film critic Robert Koehler explains, the 'construction and selection of any section [of films in a programme] immediately declares itself as, first of all, a critical statement, for the film festival programming is always and forever in its first phase an act of criticism' (2009: 82).

Transformation induced by criticism is not limited to the selection of films, but extends also to their being programmed into thematic groups, since the context in which films are displayed can instil a new understanding of a particular work in relation to a collective whole. In 2004, the Palm Springs Festival of Short Films (www.psfilmfest.org) programmed a section devoted to renowned feature film directors (Harris 2004). It is highly unlikely that the early short film work of David Lynch, Jane Campion, Spike Jonze, Francois Truffaut, Martin Scorsese, Luis Buñuel and Tim Burton had ever screened previously, or will ever screen again, together at a film festival; the uniqueness of such a presentation then ultimately influences how an audience will view each title.

Transformation ceases when the resource is finally returned to the environment (output), where it can no longer be manipulated by the film festival organisers. The time between transformation and output is determined by the properties of the resource. For example,

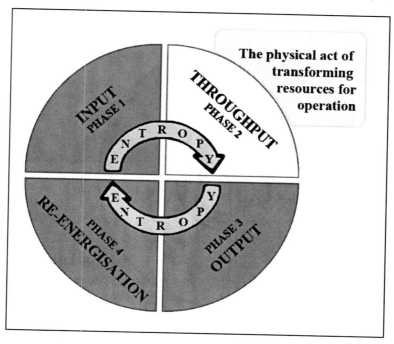

Fig. 5: Throughput/transformation – the second phase of the
Open System Paradigm. Image by A. Fischer.

the time taken between an audience member purchasing a ticket and experiencing a film might be only a matter of minutes, yet the time taken to procure that film and transform it into a screened output may have been months.

Output – Phase 3

The output phase commences when the transformed resource re-enters the environment and, again, this may be observed as occurring in a number of different ways, depending on how the transformation of the resource was accomplished. Examples of transformed resources being introduced into the environment range from the already mentioned provision of advertising or review copies to the media, through the return of a physical film to a distributor, to the specialised creation of a compact disc, like the one produced of the panel discussions that were held at and put out by Sweden's Gothenburg Film Festival (www.giff.se/us/public.html) (Gaydos 1998: 59).

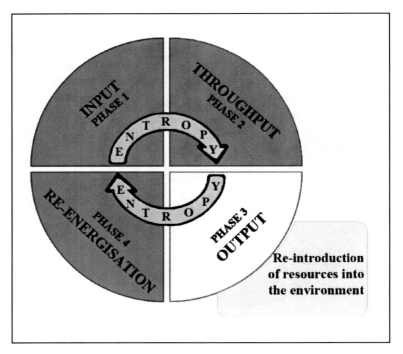

Fig. 6: Output – the third phase of the Open System Paradigm. Image by A. Fischer.

The output phase concludes when the resource has been transformed and implemented by the film festival organisers. The end of this process can be observed in such things as festival recaps. When Italy's 2009 Milan Film Festival (www.milanofilmfestival.it/eng/) issued an e-mail titled 'The festival is over – See you in 2010' that signalled not only the end of the event, but also the end of its output phase. This e-mail recapped the outcomes of the event by identifying that, for example, Laurence Thrush's *Tobira no muko* (*Left Handed*, Japan, 2008) had been awarded the prize for Best Feature Film and provided hypertext links to numerous photos and videos of the event's festivities (Milan Film Festival 2009).

It is important to note that if a transformed resource does not re-enter the environment then the output phase of operation has not been successfully completed. If a journalist were to attend a film festival and interview a guest actor without subsequently publishing the interview, the transformation from input to output would not have been achieved.

Re-energisation – Phase 4

In order to be able to replace those resources spent through operation, a film festival must re-energise its environment. Without this phase film festival continuity would be extremely difficult to achieve as operation often depletes an environment of its resources. Therefore, action must be taken by film festival organisers to ensure that future resources required for operation will be furnished, a concept called Negative Entropy (or resource replenishment, the fifth and final OSP characteristic), which will be discussed in greater detail later on. This re-energisation is best viewed as the moving of participants towards a renewed interaction with the film festival. This is not limited to previous participants, but may include new participants as well. Without an influx of new resources the film festival's performance levels would fall, if not cease altogether. It is possible for some of the outputs of film festival operation to be re-deployed as resources for input by the festival organisers, e.g. the box office returns from ticket sales can be reapplied towards the operational costs of the next film festival. However, the re-applicability of exported resources is only characteristic of a select number of tangible and service-based items. These items can be deemed generic in the sense that they can be reused for operational needs that do not require specialisation, e.g. administrative costs. For the most part, the majority of resources imported into a film festival are specialised in the sense that they cannot be reused. This single-use nature of most film festival resources has been noted by Dina Iordanova, who refers to them as 'perishable' and as having 'only a limited shelf life' (2009: 25).

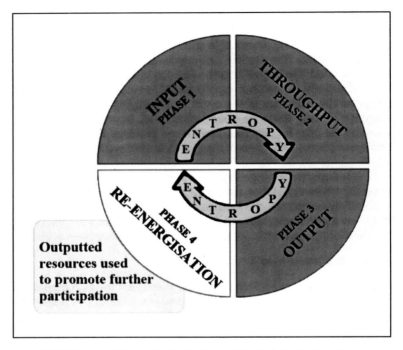

Fig. 7: Re-energisation – the fourth phase of the Open System Paradigm.
Image by A. Fischer.

This limited shelf life is often seen in the programming of commercial films, which typically have a designated number of screenings allotted per festival as dictated by the distributor or rights holder. Independent film producer Henry Rosenthal explains this aspect of exhibition further: 'As a producer, I have one special commodity – the first showing of a film. Films have almost no shelf life, no life span. Once you show a film, it's already old' (Rosenthal 2009: 35). Such a mind-set betrays this participant's primary goal of protecting his film from overexposure, but works also to the advantage of a film festival in that it promotes the uniqueness of a screening. Cathy Robinson, president of the Sydney Film Festival board from 2000 to 2005, explains this as a 'see it here, now' phenomenon that provides an important motivation for audience participation at a film festival (Robinson 2006). Stringer (2003), Cheung (2009) and Highsted (2009) also reference this phenomenon, explaining that it presents a unique social opportunity for audience participants to relish. Such motivation would undoubtedly be diminished should a film festival re-screen the same films in consecutive years.

It is important to note that motivation is not the only factor influencing the re-energisation of the environment; the availability of resources also plays a major role. As was noted earlier, film festivals are unique Open System organisations because they are sites of exhibition. Events are positioned so that they come to have a special dependency on their environment in that their role as exhibitor requires imported resources to be in their final stages of completion: a film cannot be imported like raw resources and assembled in the theatre, but must be at a stage of completion that is acceptable for an audience to watch. Noah Cowan, co-director of the Toronto International Film Festival (tiff. net/), provides insight into this situation by explaining that while Toronto may screen one or two 'works in progress', the rest of the programme consists of films that are 95 per cent to 98 per cent finished (Harris 2004a). Similarly, audience members or sources of funding may not be ready to immediately re-engage with the film festival, but may require time before participating again. So, while motivation to re-interact with a film festival may not be immediately forthcoming, strategies to re-motivate participants can occur almost instantaneously with the output of resources: a 'strike whilst the iron is hot' approach. Alternatively, months may elapse before re-motivation commences, be it in the form of an acquittal, which documents how funds supplied to a film festival were used, or as a new project proposal with critical data from the last event. Such aspects of film festival operation are contingent on the ways in which individual film festival organisers approach each of their individual resource providers.

The crucial aspect of re-energisation is that the benefits of participation must be observable; gratification must be seen to be achievable. That is, if the positive aspects of involvement are not known it is highly unlikely that potential resource providers will be motivated to participate. It is in such scenarios that awards become indispensable because, by their utilisation, film festival organisers are able to effectively control how re-energisation is perceived. For example, the Flanders International Film Festival (www.filmfestival.be) in Belgium awarded Hirokazu Koreeda's film *Dare mo shiranai* (*Nobody Knows*, Japan, 2004) the festival's Grand Prize of US$25,000 towards distribution (Graydon 2004), a case in which filmmaking participants are able to clearly observe the benefits of interaction. Mark Fishkin of the Mill Valley Film Festival recalls: 'I've had filmmakers say to us, "Well, if you gave awards, we'd be more likely to give you our film"' (Fishkin 2009c: 27). It is to their own advantage for film festival organisers to identify the benefits of participation in their own event, since 'every festival likes to point to certain films and say "it was because that film played in this festival that it

got a distribution deal, because it was a hit here, this is where it started'"
(Rosenthal 2009: 34). Such acknowledgements provide proof positive of
the benefits of involvement and may be the difference in motivating a
specific resource provider to participate in one event over another.

However, not all benefits provided by film festivals will be
interpreted as being useful. For film festival programmer Tony Rayns,
'most festival prizes have absolutely no meaning to anyone anywhere'
(Rayns 2009: 91). Producer Henry Rosenthal notes that filmmakers are
often 'exploited' by film festivals because the events rarely offer anything
more than a venue to screen their work (Rosenthal 2009: 33).

Such opinions are legitimate criticisms and come as a direct
consequence of film festivals operating as social systems. This will
be discussed further in the next chapter. For now it should be noted
that the immediate challenge of re-energisation lies in understanding
what benefits participants are most likely to value. Emile Fallaux,
former director of the International Film Festival Rotterdam (www.
filmfestivalrotterdam.com) (1991-1996) identifies one of the major
benefits for a filmmaker participating in a film festival as 'exposure to
serious criticism' (Fallaux 2009: 57). This viewpoint is shared by filmmaker
and critic Stephen Teo who viewed Chinese filmmakers' participation in
the Hong Kong International Film Festival (www.hkiff.org.hk/en/index.
php) as a 'morale booster' because they were able to submit and screen
films that did not have a commercial style (Teo 2009: 110). Each of these
situations is of course a two-edged sword for filmmakers and it is up to
the festival to promote the advantages of participation for its own ends.
In order for a film festival to achieve effective re-energisation, organisers
must be aware of, and consider the feedback from their participants.
If this does not occur then the participants may question their future
involvement, and resources an event relies on for its operation may
become unattainable.

The re-energisation phase ends with the importation of new
resources into the film festival. Thus, a complete cycle of operation
concludes when importation for the next edition begins. If film festival
organisers are unable to re-energise their environment, then this phase
of operation can be on-going, as new approaches are undertaken to try
and re-motivate the requirements for renewed interaction.

Negative entropy

Entropy, or resource depletion, plays a critical role in film festival
organisation. Re-energisation promotes negative entropy (or resource
replenishment), the fifth characteristic identified by Katz and Kahn

in the Open System. Entropy causes film festival organisers to appeal to their environment for inputs on a recurring basis; an aspect that is reaffirmed by the framework's emphasis on re-energisation. In order to fully illustrate negative entropy as the engine that drives operation, let us first look at the causes and consequences of entropy.

Entropy is the increasing disorder responsible for disorganisation and film festival demise; it occurs when resources are not replenished at a rate consistent with their output. The resultant over-expenditure, while necessary, poses the single largest threat to film festival operation. As Iordanova notes 'the main challenge for festivals is to establish a model that can function as (or at least resemble) a steady supply chain and simultaneously accommodate the realities of their discontinuity' (2009: 26).

When negative entropy occurs, an Open System is less likely to fall into disorganisation because the resources it needs to operate have been acquired. It is through the acknowledgement of entropy's role and through the development of strategies that promote negative entropy that a more comprehensive understanding of the idiosyncratic nature of film festival operation can be rationalised.

Entropy can disrupt a film festival in many unexpected ways and is a common and recurring topic raised in numerous interviews given by veteran film festival organisers. For example, Highsted explains that 'the golden rule is just to be aware of what your resources are [...] that you're not over-reaching yourself, which is very easy to do in festivals' (Highsted 2009: 50). Similarly, Bob Hawk, founder and former director of the San Fracisco-based Film Arts Festival (now part of the San Francisco Film Society www.sffs.org), expresses the need for film festival organisers to 'squeeze as much out of each day as possible', but to be conscious of when their resources are being 'maxed out' (Hawk 2009: 62).

The sporadic availability of resources also poses challenges in the time immediately following the festival. In fact, the post-operation period is one of the most vulnerable times for a film festival because the majority of resources have been utilised through operation. The likelihood of additional resource provider interaction is inherently low due to the usually extended period of time before the next event and so the potential for gratification is forestalled. This key theme is touched on by Lorena Cantrell, a former associate director of the San Francisco International Film Festival (festival.sffs.org/), who explains that volunteers rarely participate in a film festival following the cessation of operation as 'the fun's all over' (Cantrell 2009: 117). Michael Lumpkin, former director of the San Francisco International Lesbian and Gay Film Festival (www.frameline.org/festival), points out that the mistakes made

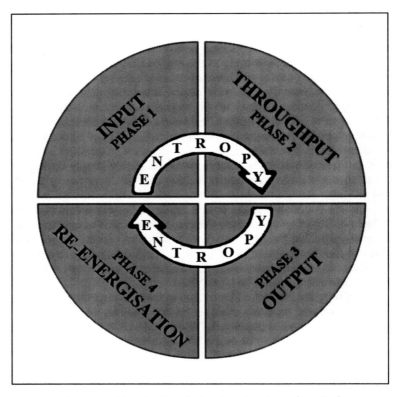

Fig. 8: Entropy drives the Open System Paradigm. Image by A. Fischer.

by film festival organisers are often compounded because they cannot be corrected until the next event, which generally means a 12-month wait (Lumpkin 2009: 128).

The inability to immediately correct operational mistakes can have a disastrous effect on film festival functionality. Fishkin explains that the 'greatest detriment to (start-up) festivals is being overly ambitious and getting yourself in a deficit position' (Fishkin 2009a: 24). Similar advice is given by Deborah Kaufman, former director of the San Francisco Jewish Film Festival (www.sfjff.org), who recommends that new festivals just 'keep the program small enough that you're not going to lose a lot of money [...] Keep it small and contain it, don't go overboard with your budget' (Kaufman 2009: 84). These are calls for the budding festival organiser to maintain control over the entropy of their event.

Fig. 9: The film festival as a bucket full of water. Image by Nick Tran Van Vinh.

The concept of entropy is perhaps most effectively visualised when a film festival is pictured as a bucket containing water.

It is the job of film festival organisers to get just the right amount of water to fill the bucket (i.e. maintain resources such as funding, films, audience members, etc.) so that the event can operate. However, the very act of operation requires the use of resources, which inevitably causes the water level to drop. This is entropy – the disorganisation that ensues due to the very operation of the event – usually caused by the depletion of finances, films or participation.

The image of a leaking bucket shows three major types of entropy draining a film festival.

Effective film festival management ensures that an event loses only as much water (resources) through operation as the bucket (festival) contains; no need for top-ups. Therefore, decisions and actions that will overextend the festival's resource pool and that see the creation of flows

Fig. 10: The film festival as a bucket with three types of entropic leaks. Image by Nick Tran Van Vinh.

29

too large for the operational capacity of a film festival to be sustainable, must be avoided. The transient nature of festival operation manifests itself in a continual need and effort to replenish resources such as funding, films, volunteers and festival guests, in a staggered, contingent manner designed to meet the appropriate demands of operation at suitable times.

The three major types of entropy to keep in check are financially driven entropy, operations-driven entropy and participation-driven entropy.

Financially driven entropy

Financially driven entropy stems from the economic requirements that occur during operation and includes the costs associated with programming, guests and operations. Financial resources invested in a festival include monetary contributions as well as in-kind contributions, such as the donation of goods or services. Both of these resource types are equally important to operation, since in-kind contributions may enable the film festival to make a profit by relieving organisers of the need to pay any overhead costs towards, for example, a local volunteer dance troupe or for the use of donated venues and equipment.

When a financial resource is no longer available, film festival organisers must make structural adjustments in order to curb the impacts of the entropy that result. When, for example, in 2009 the Bangkok International Film Festival (www.bangkokfilm.org) had its budget slashed by Bt120 million (US$4 million), organisers compensated for the lack of funding by reducing the total number of programmed films and by shifting their attention away from titles that were typically more expensive due to their transportation and hire costs (Parinyaporn 2009). This served to reverse the entropy of the festival and allowed it to function at a more modest but sustainable level.

The financial budgets of film festivals vary from event to event, yet there is an observed standard pool of money from which the majority of financial-based resources originate. Film festival practitioners Cathy Robinson (Robinson 2006), Simon Field (Field 2009), Emile Fallaux (Tanner 2009) and Deborah Kaufman (Tanner 2009), explain that their respective events' financial bases are evenly distributed between three distinct funding sources: government grants, private sponsorship and earned income, e.g. ticket sales.

This diversification of resource supplies enables the film festival organisers to avoid an over-reliance on one specific source of funding. As explained by Kaufman, 'Our stability and our strength has to do with our (mix of funding) – it's 1/3 earned income, 1/3 donations and 1/3 grants' (Kaufman 2009: 82; parentheses in original). Such stability and strength stems from the likelihood that the event will still be able to function even if a financial contributor should not participate. In 2004, for example, the Montréal World Film Festival (www.ffm-montreal.org/) lost over C$1.5 million dollars (US$1.49 million) in funding support from its Canadian government sponsors (Kelly 2004a). However, the 2005 edition of the festival was still able to operate on the financial support received from private sponsors, including Air Canada, AGF and Visa; and by 2007, the organisers were able to reactivate the government public funding stream (that is, to re-energise the environment) and increase it nearly fivefold from C$190,000 (US$188,000) in 2006 to C$850,000 (US$840,000) (Kelly 2007).

Financial resources are generally acquired prior to the facilitation of the physical event, and so film festival organisers engage and interact with finance-based resource providers before any others. Some film festival organisers may use the participation of a key individual, such as an Hollywood actor, to make involvement more appealing. For the stars it is usually a case of 'show me the gratitude' in the shape of expensive gifts, hotel rooms, food and drink, etc., before they will take their billing. The timing of such engagements is often the result of the financial calendar, so proposals may be submitted to private businesses in order to take advantage of new sponsorship opportunities; or, in the case of government funding, to correspond with bureaucratic assessment periods, which can take anywhere from one to six months.

That much of the funding allocated to a film festival is designated for specific applications and is therefore restricted in terms of how it can be used, provides an additional challenge in terms of financially-driven entropy. Money, and especially money provided by a government agency, is often supplied on the condition that it is used only to facilitate certain approved activities stipulated in the funding proposal. Larry Horne, founder and former director of the Los Angeles Gay and Lesbian Film Festival (www.outfest.org), recalls that a grant he received from the California Council for the Humanities had to be used to stage 'a conference around the issues of gay and lesbian identity in the media' (Horne 2009: 102). The restrictive nature of such funding allocations means that a film festival can experience financial entropy even though it has money available. Situations like that often require organisers to make payment-related sacrifices in order for money to be reallocated to those areas crucial to functionality. Fishkin notes that the film festival organisers' salaries 'didn't become stable until somewhere between our fifth and eighth years' (Fishkin 2009c: 26). According to Gretchen Elsner-Sommer, the organisers of the U.S.-based Women in the Director's Chair

Film Festival (www.widc.org) were not paid until the festival's eighth year of operation (Elsner-Sommer 2009: 100).

Operations-driven entropy

Operations-driven entropy stems from the use of resources such as films and venues, which exist in finite quantities in the environment and are consequently of limited availability. These resources are required for operation and often have the 'limited shelf life' previously referred to, both in terms of their appeal, and in their incorporation into the film festival. An example comes with Parinyaporn Pajee's (2009) report on the Bangkok International Film Festival which could not secure theatres during its scheduled dates of operation, with the result that the event was moved to a time when venues were available. Another example of a rapidly encroaching threat of operations-driven entropy is provided by J. David Slocum, who relates the Zanzibar International Film Festival's (www.zanzibar.org/ziff) experience of the closing of the African 'island's last three commercial cinemas' (2009: 141). Such a situation is a justifiable cause for alarm for the event's organisers since an absence of a venue makes film festival functionality logistically impossible.

The programming of certain films can often be similarly affected by such things as distributor release dates, and by bookings that conflict with other film festivals. Peranson provides insight into the challenges that arise between time and resource availability with his observation that most 'of the time there is only one English-subtitled print of a [newly-released] film in the world – a film can only be in one place at one time' (2009: 25). The reality that the resources required for operation are rarely available upon demand contributes to the unique organisational structure of film festivals. Such a contingency as this stems, once again, from the film festival's status as a unique Open System organisation; a social system that is a site of exhibition, subject to a range of unique operational considerations. In this case, it is the availability of a finalised product.

Unique to each festival is not only the type, but also the degree of operations-driven entropy. Not all film festivals require the same number of films for programming – the first Durban Film Festival only showed seven titles (Kriedemann 2009) while the Berlin International Film Festival's public programme regularly includes up to 400 films (Berlin Film Festival 2009a). Each event has a critical mass of resources that must be utilised. This critical mass is often indicative of the goals or ambitions of the film festival organisers, but may also be linked to funding, since many government organisations will sometimes stipulate that a certain number and type of film must be included in order to fulfil requirements for payment.

That a film festival requires a certain amount of resources for operation makes this type of entropy especially challenging to counter since the environment may not contain enough resources to meet a particular film festival's needs. As programmer James Quintín explains, the programme of a contemporary 'mid-sized festival (let's say, about 200 films) is equivalent to what one used to be able to see throughout the year in first-run cinemas' (2009: 40; parentheses in original) and this expansion of programming has a dramatic effect on how film festivals are able to operate. For example, film director and critic Mark Cousins explains that although 3,000 films are produced yearly, 'at most, only 150 of the annual 3,000 films are of real artistic merit' (2009: 155). Similar sentiments are expressed by Robert Koehler who further narrows the field by identifying the number of 'films that truly matter' produced in any one year as being under 40 (2009: 87), and Simon Field who lowers that number even further to between 10 and 20 'good-to-great' films produced annually (2009: 67).

With thousands of festivals in operation each year this is a situation that places enormous stress on film festival organisers. It creates a competitive environment between events, that is further exacerbated by the limited windows of opportunity there are to actually screen a film before it is commercially released. This effective 'starvation of resources' has a trickle-down effect, as Field explains:

> The essential point in all of this is that there are only so many crucial and necessary films to go around, and smaller festivals assuming that they can premiere important or even just quality films are generally deluding themselves. (2009: 88)

Operations-driven entropy (though not identified or named as such) has been and continues to be a major cause for concern among all FIAPF (Fédération Internationale des Associations de Producteurs de Films / International Federation of Film Producers Associations) accredited A-list film festivals. Cousins' previous numbering of 150 films of merit is made more complicated by the fact that

> To qualify, each of the 12 [A-listed film festivals] must have a competition section containing at least 14 world-premiered films. So, each year, the A listers alone have at least 168 slots for new films to fill which means, in theory, swallowing up all 150 of the good movies of the year. (2009: 155-6; emphasis in original)

A similar observation is made by Quintín who confirms that A-list requirements are essentially flawed because 'there are not enough films to premiere in order to fulfil expectations, since the producers all attempt to get their films into Cannes first and secondly into Venice or Berlin' (Porton 2009: 42). In 2004, FIAPF solved this entropic problem by revising the rules to reflect the realities of film availability (Masters 2004).

Operations-driven entropy also influences the decision-making process of film festival organisers in ways that can be observed in such things as venue selection and engagement. The availability of venues is always a concern when organising a film festival, and some of the more original methods of overcoming this entropy-driven challenge include modifying other, abundant resources into venues. Lateral thinking by Canada's Whistler Film Festival (whistlerfilmfestival.com) enabled it to create a projection surface made entirely of snow, and the British-based Leeds International Film Festival (www.leedsfilm.com) made a similar innovative use of the façade of The Queen's Hotel as a projection surface (Cowie 2002: 355).

Understanding the 'primacy of a venue in the study of festivals' enables a better understanding of 'the various efforts festivals make in order to overcome the shortcomings of their idiosyncratic and limited supply chain' (Iordanova 2009: 26). Many of these idiosyncrasies become costly: hiring a venue that is well-suited to both the needs of the audience and the technical aspects of projection can be extremely expensive. In fact, Jim Yee, founder of the San Francisco International Asian American Film Festival (festival.asianamericanmedia.org) emphatically warns others to be 'very cautious of any kind of venue' (Yee 2009: 142). Just because it was built does not mean that they will come. An audience is not guaranteed and film festival organisers must be aware that money spent on venue hire may not be recovered in box office income. Gary Meyer, co-founder of Landmark Theatres and co-director of the Telluride Film Festival, has much to say on this matter from the perspective of the theatre owner:

> Whatever price we [the theatre] ultimately decide upon for the rental of the theater, you're [the festival organiser] responsible for that... I don't want you coming back to me begging for a reduction in terms. I can't do that when you haven't sold enough tickets. (Meyer 2009: 72-3)

Participation-driven entropy

Participation-based resources are vulnerable to entropy because, by definition, they require physical attendance or participation at the event. Participation comes in the form of the attendance of audience members, entertainment reporters and filmmakers, for example, who are all required to attend in order to fulfil the requirements of input, transformation and output in an Open System. The physical participation of these particular groups is a means of validating the relevance of a film festival through audience statistics and media articles, as is the recorded and transmitted attendance of film industry icons, which is often used as proof of an event's appeal (and which can be used to motivate the future participation of other resource providers). The Slovakia-based Art Film Fest (www.artfilmfest.sk) is just one example of a festival that was eager to boast of a 'record attendance' at its 2009 edition, and similar observations validating the importance of participation can be found on the Internet database *filmfestivalworld.com* (2008), which actually lists participation of three types: attendance, media attendance and accredited industry attendance.

It is participation-based entropy that sees participants 'burnout' (Highsted 2009: 47; Cantrell 2009: 116), be they audience members, film industry personnel or volunteers. Ron Henderson, executive/artistic director of the Denver International Film Festival (DIFF) (www.denverfilm. org/festival) for 30 years, equates the taxing effect of film festival operation on a festival's 'human resources' with that which lessens the value of 'dollar resources' (Henderson 2009: 124). The DIFF is particularly fortunate, he says, because it has a 'very low turnover' of those seasonal workers who contribute to the continuity of the event's operation (Ibid.). The difficulty film festivals face in sustaining volunteer support over an extended period of time can often be laid at the feet of burnout. Aware of this, the Toronto International Film Festival deliberately begins the slow recruitment of its volunteers at the beginning of May, with peak enlisting coming in time to match the festival's operation in September (SECOR 2004: 27). Most film festival organisers plan volunteer involvement to correspond with periods of high activity so as to use these human resources to maximum effect. Those who input their volunteered time and effort to the festival often see their work transformed into a box office consideration and output as free attendance. This is negative entropy in action.

The characteristic period-based functioning of film festivals brings an additional effect of this specific type of entropy into play. As previously mentioned, film festivals must allow their environments to re-energise (Phase 4) before they are able to import additional resources for inputting. The fact that this re-energising may itself take a while means that the assemblage of an operational structure for a film festival must not take too long to accomplish. Some operational techniques manifest in the 'down times' or 'seasonal work' characteristics indicative of most film festivals, during which time

> cash flows are tight and you have to develop your year-round staff very slowly [...] So you wind up trying to make do with a limited year-round staff covering a lot of different positions, and then you bring on people seasonally. (Fishkin 2009c: 25)

SECOR Consulting reports that both the Atlantic (www.atlanticfilm.com) and the Vancouver International Film Festivals have a permanent staff of just eight or nine employees that increases to '70 during the festival period' (2004: 26).

Acknowledgement of the three types of entropy provides a comprehensive way of approaching an understanding of the resource-driven conditions under which film festival operation occurs. It is important to note though that these specific types are actually three parts of a whole. That is, entropy is a completely disorganising force and the delineation of these three types of resource depletion is merely employed to present the information in a more meaningful manner. Through the use of the OSP, the importation of resources can be seen as a necessary functional aspect used to combat entropy, to promote negative entropy and ultimately enable sustainable operation. It is typical for film festivals to attempt to slow entropy by limiting organisational activity and utilising resources that may have been stored for such a reason; to hibernate. Such operational techniques result in the down times experienced by the majority of film festivals. By entering a reduced operational period, film festival organisers are able to maintain their operation during lulls in importation, effectively forestalling the disorganising effects of entropy until new resources are secured.

The aim of this chapter has been to encourage film festival practitioners to look at their festival as something other than a film festival; as a system of events that is logically and necessarily connected to its environment. Viewing an event in this way promotes a rational understanding of film festival operation, but it is not without its disadvantages. Chief among these is the fact that the framework places the majority of its understanding on the structure and function of film festivals rather than on the day-to-day tasks of getting a festival organised. It can be argued that such a pragmatic examination has the potential to oversimplify the notion of resources, reducing it to a discussion of the monetary at the expense of the social aspects of operation. But the social aspects of interaction cannot be quantified into a structural framework because they are never truly known. That is, the beliefs, perceptions and motivations that drive resource providers to participate in a film festival are individual to each participant and what inspires one particular person to interact with the festival in one particular way may cause another to totally disengage from the event.

Successful film festivals are repeated cycles of an Open System. For Katz and Kahn, there is 'no anatomy to a social system', and an organisation is only represented by the occurrence of 'events or happenings rather than of physical parts' (1978: 36). The four cyclical phases of the Open System Paradigm framework are entirely based on those events and happenings that connect resources throughout the course of a film festival and that are critical to its operation. By connecting the dots of festival operation, by following what happens to individual resources during their four phases of interaction with a festival – input, transformation, output and re-energisation – the organiser becomes much more aware of the motivations, perceptions and beliefs of the participants with whom they engage, and so are more able to work towards their gratification – the subject of the next chapter.

Chapter 3
The Science of Success:
Eight Strategies That Increase
Film Festival Attractiveness

Few phrases are more commonly uttered by film festival organisers than 'this year's event was a success'. Whether it is box office activity, the number of world premières or the presence of Hollywood actors, there are always select aspects of operation on which film festival organisers will focus as proof of their event's importance and validity. For the most part, such assertions of an event's success generally go unchallenged. In 2009 a press release issued by the Tourism Authority of Thailand proclaimed the Bangkok International Film Festival to have been a 'success'. According to influential film critic Kong Rithdee, however, the press release had overstated things, especially as the festival subsequently failed to take place the next year (Kong Rithdee 2009: 129). Such verbal manipulation is common and can even be expected to some degree, because a festival's future success depends on its reputation and perception by evaluators. As film festivals are social organisations, participants' pre-agreed involvement could have direct consequences for the availability of many resources required for their operation.

This need for the pre-agreed involvement causes social systems to be 'contrived' and 'imperfect' because the foundations for interaction are 'anchored in the attitudes, perceptions, beliefs, motivations, habits, and expectations of human beings' (Katz and Kahn 1978: 37), rather than in physical necessity. The availability of films and funding from external sources cannot be assumed, because, while participation may be predicted, it cannot be made certain. People are fickle. Framing an event in the best possible light becomes critical in order to enable lobbying for the most highly sought-after resources. This is an aspect of film festival management that festival director Grady Hendrix likens to 'a delicate psychological game' (2005).

The seemingly ubiquitous use of the term 'success' leads to situations where actual, successful film festival operation becomes increasingly difficult to recognise, and the perceptions of resource providers become skewed towards particular indicators. For example, Craig Alexander implies that in order for a film festival to successfully operate, organisers must sell a critical mass of tickets; both the Montréal

World Film Festival and the Toronto International Film Festival are therefore deemed successful because they sell 'around ¼ million seats every year' (1997: 17).

Certainly, financial information, such as the bottom line profit or loss for a film festival, should be taken into account when evaluating its viability. An inability to make a profit is indicative of financial entropy as it manifests itself in those operational costs associated with standard functionality – venue hire, print hire, publicity, etc. – which lower the financially-driven threshold of an event. Yet it is important that all financial information is understood within the larger operational context and is communicated appropriately, and to the appropriate individuals, so as to avoid any misconceptions regarding the vitality of the event. Simply stating that a film festival is not a success because it is unable to generate a net profit may mean that the successful function of the event as a cultural platform has been overlooked.

In fact, the majority of film festivals do not make money and the idea that a film festival is a profit-making venture is fundamentally flawed. As writer and social commentator Sambolgo Bangré explains, 'festivals that are financed essentially by their own takings are few and far between.' (1996: 158). Even the Vancouver International Film Festival, which reportedly generates more income from ticket sales than Toronto, Montréal or the Atlantic Film Festival, is still dependent upon 'substantial cash sponsorship revenues' (SECOR 2004: 48). According to producer and film festival director Aleksandr Rodnyansky, the Russia-based Kinotavr Film Festival (www.kinotavr.ru/en) 'is absolutely loss-making' (Gavrilova 2009: 19), but it still operates. This is a situation familiar to two of the world's most prominent film festivals, the Sundance Film Festival (Smith 1999) and the Toronto International Film Festival (Johnson 2000), each of which suffered major financial losses in their initial years of operation.

Tom Di Mara, former executive director of Frameline (www. frameline.org), notes that the economic challenges of film festival operation often determine the types of organisations that will facilitate the events, because 'festivals are not lucrative. If festivals made a lot of money, they'd be commercial, more profit companies would do them, but they're always done by non-profit [companies] because there's no money there!' (Di Mara 2009: 132). Yet, by opening itself up to such assessments of success, a festival also falls prey to the claws of criticism. This is most often evident when an event is compared to its own previous editions. According to Geoffrey Gilmore, former director of the Sundance Festival and current director of Tribeca Enterprises, successive Sundance festivals were differentiated according only to their ticket sales relative to each other, with 'one festival [being] regarded by media pundits as a success, the other as a failure' (2009). Having to live up to one's own publicity can be a frustrating exercise.

Perhaps the most difficult aspect of this situation is that, for much of the time, film festival organisers have very little control over the quality or type of input that might be on offer in any given year. As sites of exhibition, reliant on the works produced by others, festivals must face instances where the quality of the only films available for programming is inferior to that of previous years. There are, of course, methods for framing such films via programming notes, scheduling and secondary activities like workshops, but such actions require additional time and resources from festival organisers: time and resources that could be spent more 'profitably' elsewhere.

The best method for judging the success of a film festival is by examining the re-energisation of the environment that occurs after the event. The operation of a film festivals follows a pattern that addresses aspects of programming, funding acquisition, volunteer involvement, marketing and the like, in an identifiable cycle (or cycles) of activity. In an effort to discuss the various aspects of film festival operation, SECOR Consulting identified eight major phases of film festival operation – 'planning, sourcing, selection, organization, programming, marketing, delivery and assessment' – that occur in 'a circular process, since the end of each festival marks the start of organizing the next one, with the results of the year ended providing key input for the following year's planning' (2004: 29). The details of such a cycle or cycles are unique to each individual film festival at particular moments of its operation and are highly dependent upon such detailed variables as employment contracts, funding opportunities and alignment with the festival circuit.

It can be difficult for an existing film festival to identify the exact point at which activities commence and conclude. One of the most obvious markers of film festival activity is the yearly call for entries inviting potential participants with films eligible for programming to submit their work to the festival. But often film festival organisers begin planning and making arrangements for the next event or events – by issuing invitations for special guests, for example – so far in advance that it occurs simultaneously with a period of activity in the current festival. That is, arrangements for a film festival to be held in 2014 more than likely began early in 2013.

Through their cycle of operation, film festivals aim to perpetuate their value to the participants upon whom they rely for their resources. Distribution deals that occur at film festivals, such as the 'buying frenzy' which took place at Sundance in 1996 and at which more films were sold in six days than in the whole of the previous year and a half (Gilmore in

Biskind 2004: 228), have the ability to re-energise the environment with the potential for gratification that participants may use as motivation for their subsequent involvement. Gilmore explains that such an event 'inspired the kind of buzz and interest where the industry and filmmaking community says, "That is great, this is a door, something I can walk through"' (Ibid.). More films means more opportunities for gratification and, ultimately, a greater programming selection from which the festival may choose.

Similar, but less publicised reactivation can occur with funding. In the majority of instances in which film festivals receive money from a government funding body, the festival is required to submit an acquittal form after the event that details how the funding was spent and ultimately contributed to the event. If such an acquittal is successful, that is, if it is approved by the holders of the governmental purse strings, the festival then holds greater likelihood that future funding from that source can be obtained. Should the final report not be submitted or be judged as unsatisfactory, then the converse is more likely and the festival will need to look elsewhere for its future funding.

By and large, the organiser has little or no ability to change how people external to the event actually view the film festival, so when operational decisions are made based on a festival's ability to complete an operational cycle rather than on the number of film premières or the calibre of the glitterati scattered across the red carpet, the potential for an event's longevity is drastically improved. This is because by concentrating on systemic issues, the attention of the organiser is drawn away from distracting minutiae and directed solely towards the perpetuation of the festival itself. Equating operational viability (or success) with the number of years of operation is already acknowledged as a gauge of success. Festivals are constantly at pains to draw attention to the number of years or editions they have operated: Elley refers to the '10th anni [anniversary]' of the Pusan Film Festival' (2005); Shael Stolberg makes particular note of the fact that the German-based Max Ophüls Preis Film Festival (www.max-ophuels-preis.de) was 'founded in 1980' (2000: 23); and Will Tizard describes the Karlovy Vary Film Festival (www.kviff.com/en/news) as having achieved its '40th edition' (2005) in a context that is meant to convey approval and optimism. By addressing the concept of cycles rather than the intricacies of actual operation when assessing a festival's success, organisers are better able to meet the challenges that the need for resource importation places on an event. The devil is in the detail and it can be a hellish task to address the particulars of operation while trying to maintain a grasp on an indeterminate whole.

There are very few certainties when it comes to film festival management, but there are certain strategies that can genuinely influence the likelihood of external participation. And these strategies owe their existence to the nature of film festivals as Open Systems, as systems which rely on the importation of resources based on participant motivation, which itself originates in the gratification that participants receive from interaction (Parsons 1951: 6). While resources can never be guaranteed, their importation may be positively influenced by the prospect of a beneficial return as a result of participation.

This book delineates eight different strategies used by film festival organisers to promote stable resource importation. The strategies are arranged in no particular order and although some strategies may be observed to be more widely used than others, no single strategy is proposed as being the best or foremost; the efficacy of each is contingent on the particular circumstances of a particular festival at a particular stage of its operation. It is also important to note that many of these strategies are interconnected and that the total number of strategies implemented is a unique choice faced by individual film festival organisers. That is, while their implementation occurs on a wide scale across a whole festival, those specific strategies deployed by each event, and their timings, are ultimately dictated by what is considered to be most effective for motivating participation in each particular case. Once again, it is important to point out that this is a book about how to look at film festival operation rather than specific instruction on how to operate a festival.

Strategy One: Build Alliances

A co-operative alliance is a partnership formed between a film festival and another organisation based on reciprocal benefits for both organisations, which can include such things as the sharing of resources, joint applications for funding and/or cross-promotional activities through media and contact databases. This reciprocity-based understanding is congruent with scholar Becky Starnes' observation that strategically, such an 'alliance may be defined as a "relationship developed between parties to achieve common interests"' (2000: 17).

The executive director of the Vancouver International Film Festival, Alan Franey, raises the idea of piggybacking resources with other organisations and explains that co-operation between a first-time film festival and entities such as theatres, other festivals and libraries, is an effective means of 'getting something off the ground' (Franey 2009: 30). Such piggybacking can be seen with the first edition of Norway's Bergen International Film Festival (www.biff.no/2010/en), which was held as part of the 'celebration of Bergen as European City of Culture' (Cowie 2002: 355). It is, however, important to note that this strategy need not only be used during film festival formation, but that it can also occur across the operation of a film festival. This is a point expanded upon by film festival director Gretchen Elsner-Sommer, who explains that 'it's very important to collaborate, not only with other media arts organizations, and other film and video festivals, but with community groups, educational groups, with a lot of different people' (Elsner-Sommer 2009: 97).

Most co-operative alliances see film festivals performing a film-related function, e.g. the organisers of the Denver International Film Festival help to facilitate the Aurora Asian Film Festival (auroraasian.org) in conjunction with the Aurora Asian/Pacific Community Partnership and the City of Aurora (at least until the partnership ended in 2010). In this type of co-operative alliance the film festivals are identified as film authorities and are therefore in charge of film-based activities.

In order for a co-operative alliance to be entered into, there must be no threat of competition. That is, each entity must be seen as performing different services that do not encroach upon the availability of resources for the other. Such a relationship once existed between film festivals and art house cinemas according to critic Adrian Martin, but the co-operation was soon replaced by competitiveness over programming:

> For a long time, [film festivals and arthouse cinemas] existed in symbiosis, and events moved in lockstep: arthouse distributors would preview their latest acquisitions at a high-profile festival screening [...] This relationship often indeed became rather too close for comfort, with certain festivals coming to increasingly resemble vast, compliant 'showcases' for upcoming arthouse product. (2009: 105)

It is important to note that when it does occur, such competition is driven largely by geography and so it is still common for prints to be shared between film festivals and art house cinemas that do not have an overlapping target audience, as a quick hunt around the on-line film programming forums will reveal.

The sharing of resources is common between film festivals, too. Slovenia's Kino Otok (Cinema Island) (www.isolacinema.org/en) is 'part of an informal association of similarly interested and same-sized international film festivals with which they sometimes share prints and travel expenses, occasionally develop programming ideas, etc.' (Möller 2009: 145). Such co-operation serves a dual purpose. Firstly, it enables film festival organisers to keep the operational costs associated with print transportation low – a very important aspect identified by Hope (2005) in her discussion of the early development of and alliances between the Melbourne International and Sydney Film Festivals. Secondly, partnerships promote an efficiency of business that is likely to encourage participation. Co-operation between film festival organisers motivates resource providers like distributors and sales agents to participate by proving to be an efficient method for moving a product such as a film through the festival 'supply chain' (Iordanova 2009: 26).

The majority of resource-based co-operation between film festivals occurs when the events take place in different locations. For example, the San Francisco International Asian American Film Festival is able to share programming with its 'sister festivals' in cities such as San Diego, Seattle, Chicago, Los Angeles, Minneapolis, New York and Washington, D.C. (Gore 2001: 321), largely because these places are far away enough from each other to not affect each other's ability to attract audiences and sponsors.

There are, however, instances in which film festivals from the same city are able to work together. Scholar Joshua Gamson discusses the co-operative endeavour between two lesbian and gay film festivals in New York. The New York Lesbian and Gay Film Festival (www.mixnyc.org) and The New York Lesbian and Gay Experimental Film Festival (newfest.slated.com/2011) are able to collaborate due to the large size of the lesbian and gay populations within the city, or, as Gamson explains, 'New York is one of the few places where a gay and lesbian audience can be divided' (1996: 244). This situation works to the advantage of both events, as the organisers are able to set up a 'division of labour' which includes open discussions about programming and collaboration that 'not only reduces conflict between the festivals, it also allows each festival to go about its own business without tremendous internal conflict' (Ibid.). Such a situation is rare if two film festivals are competing for the same resources in the same city or area.

Co-operative alliances give film festivals access to more potential resources than if they operated in isolation. For example, filmmaker, scholar and film festival organiser Yu Shan Huang explains how the Taiwan-based Women's Film Festival (www.wmw.com.tw/en) co-operates with groups such as the 'Women's Rights Promotion Association, Public Television, the Alliance of Community Mother, and the Women Rescue and Support Association' and so is able to reach a broader audience (2003: 157). Similarly, writer Raymond J. Haberski notes how organisers of the New York Film Festival identified the benefits of 'joining forces' with the city's largest film society as a means of increasing the likelihood of a 'large popular turnout' (2001: 155).

Co-operation also enables a film festival to be seen as an event, thus allowing more opportunities for drawing in participation than would ordinarily be available. At the second edition of the UK-based

Royal Anthropological Institute's International Festival of Ethnographic Film (raifilmfest.org.uk), for example, a book was published discussing the results of a conference held in conjunction with the film festival (Crawford and Turton 1992). Similarly, Beauchamp and Béhar make special note of a fashion show held during the 1947 Cannes Film Festival at which the first 'Miss Festival' was crowned (1992: 165). The auxiliary nature of these events is useful in attracting participants who might otherwise forego involvement with a film festival, and this additional participation can be especially useful in motivating sponsors who may not have an immediate connection with film, but who are interested in what the film festival represents because of the co-operation of another organisation. In that vein, the U.S.-based Small Pictures International Film Festival (no URL) annually selected a charity to which the proceeds from the festival would be donated (Gore 2001: 328).

Strategy Two: Get the Timing Right

Timing, as a strategy, refers to the operational positioning of a film festival at a specified period during the calendar year in order to overcome financial and operations-driven entropy. More simply put, it is vital to hold a festival at the best possible time of year. Positioning the event in this way is considered strategic because film festival organisers are able to take advantage of regularly scheduled occurrences such as distributor release patterns, other film festivals and even of cyclical funding opportunities. SECOR Consulting found the timing of a festival to be 'so important that some festivals and markets change theirs in an attempt to increase attendance or to enhance their positioning vis-à-vis the competition' (2004: 19). Timing is a key consideration when film festival organisers are assessing the best conditions under which to conduct film festival operation.

This strategy was first developed, consciously or not, by the organisers of the Venice International Film Festival in 1932, the first festival to be 'organized on a regular basis' (de Valck 2007: 47). The recurring operation of Venice was the result of its affiliation with a long-running, annual and overarching event, the Venice Arts Biennale, to which the film festival was originally attached as a means of extending the tourist season (Ibid. 76). So this strategy of timing allowed the festival to partake in the further strategy of co-operative alliance; piggybacking.

Timing can enhance the importation of resources by allowing film festival organisers to structure events around any potential opportunities for increased levels of participation. For example, San Francisco's Cine Acción Cine Latino (no URL) was held during Hispanic Heritage Month (Gore 2001: 267). Positioning the film festival at this time enabled the organisers to form co-operative alliances with ethnic community members and organisations more likely to be proactive in their involvement due to the overall raised level of awareness.

The timing of operation can also provide a film festival with greater programming opportunities. Dimitris Kerkinos, director of the Balkan Film Survey at the Thessaloniki International Film Festival (www.filmfestival.gr) in Greece, identifies the event as having an advantage over other film festivals in the Mediterranean because its end-of-the-year position allows organisers to programme a 'more complete picture of the annual Balkan production' (2009: 175). Similarly, the Tokyo International Film Festival (www.tiff-jp.net/en) changed its dates of operation from September to November because this new timing enabled the film festival to 'get more films that would be in theaters for the end-of-the-year holiday season' (Herskovitz 1998: 166).

This strategy also serves to communicate the territory occupied by a particular event so as to avoid any conflict or trespassing by rival festivals. For example, Peter Biskind explains how the scheduling of the Utah-based Slamdance Film Festival (www.slamdance.com) in America, which coincided with Sundance, was not 'graciously' accepted by the latter festival's organisers, who ultimately compared Slamdance to a 'parasite' (2004: 229). Given that the rival event's physical presence was observed to draw potential resources such as audience members and media attention away from Sundance, such a likeness is appropriate, if somewhat harsh. Janet Harbord discusses the timing of film festival operation in greater detail, noting the influences that a 'limited schedule of screenings and ticket sales, the last-minute release of the full programme, and the connected events surrounding screenings' all have on the various participants (2009: 40-1).

From an Open System Paradigm perspective the designation of a date of operation clearly communicates to resource providers the point at which the film festival will be seeking more and different resources. So, a call for entries is conducted in the months leading up to operation, allowing time for film festival organisers to programme and plan event logistics.

The timing of operation is similarly important to the influx of participation-based resources – audience members, media, filmmakers – and *Variety* is most particular about stating either the date or duration of a film festival in nearly all of its festival reports. Such an emphasis on dates obviously serves to alert potential attendees who are unfamiliar with the event as to when the film festival will be held. But the designation of a specific operational period also provides participants with a necessary point of reference regarding when the re-energisation of new resources must be completed should they wish to interact. For example, film critic Michael Fox explains how filmmakers will 'target' the particular date of a film festival and plan their production schedule: 'They think, "If we start now, can we get this ready for Sundance? If we miss Sundance, will we have it ready for Berlin?"' (Fox 2009: 148).

The impact of a strategically scheduled film festival also enables the participants such as Hollywood distributors to better prepare for, and to ultimately benefit more from an event because they can incorporate that event into their own business structures. Beauchamp and Béhar explain how a screening at Cannes factors into the publicity of a film's commercial release schedule:

> The primary reason to be in Cannes centers on publicity, the final decision to go revolves around the film's release date. There are three categories: a movie that has had a full run in the States, one premièred internationally immediately before or after the U.S. release, and one with a release date still several months away. (1992: 223)

The fact that a film festival's date can influence the motivation of certain highly sought-after resource providers promotes the idea that there are certain times that will allow film festivals better access to resources. According to Robert Koehler, only Cannes, Toronto, Venice and Berlin are 'ever able to generally secure the films they actually want' (2009: 82). A similar statement is made by Simon Field, former director of the International Film Festival Rotterdam, who explains that 'Venice, Berlin, Cannes can scoop up the best films' while the Montréal, San Sébastian and Karlovy Vary festivals get the 'scraps and leftovers' (Field 2009: 70).

Beauchamp and Béhar note that the positioning of Cannes in the northern autumn is 'seen as increasing the odds of drawing the American and studio-produced films' (1992: 365) to the festival. This increase of the odds of securing a particular type of programming is primarily the result of the scheduled release dates implemented by distributors: 'The "Bible on Release Dates" still dictated that summer was a horrible time to release a low-budget or "thoughtful" film. That time was set aside for hardware blockbusters' (Ibid.).

Since there are patterns of resource availability according to which film festivals organisers must consider establishing their operational structure, it is very likely that conflict will arise between film festival organisers who may feel that their territory on the calendar has been encroached upon by potential rivals. As Kerkinos explains, 'with such a proliferation [of festivals] it's inevitable that the competition between festivals has increased dramatically, especially between those which share similar profiles' (2009: 168). Such a situation took place in 2003 when the Montréal World Film Festival moved its operational date back five days, causing it to overlap with both the Venice and Toronto festivals (Poirier 2003). One of the stipulations of FIAPF accreditation is a non-conflicting date of operation, so when Montréal moved its dates, it violated this rule and thereby lost its 'A-list' status (Ibid.). Accusations flew about personal 'ill will' between the organisers, Montréal's Serge Losique and Venice's Moritz de Hadeln (Gaydos 2005). Such a threat only arises if the film festivals actually share the same or similar resource providers, although such territorial 'cat fights' among film festivals are common when public money is given to one film festival and not to another (Cousins 2009: 156).

Of the estimated thousands of film festivals organised annually, FIAPF only has governance over 49 (2009), and many non-FIAPF film festivals are understood to be important – e.g. Telluride, Tribeca, Busan, Vancouver and Sundance. So, regardless of the existence of rules, it is inevitable that there will be some crossover between festivals of similar size, stature and focus. Todd McCarthy identifies Sundance as able to take 'advantage of its position as the first major festival of the calendar year' to get 'the jump on both Rotterdam and Berlin' (2004). However, this jump is downplayed by Geoffrey Gilmore, who describes the similarity in programming between the three festivals as only overlapping 'somewhat' (Ibid.), thus enabling them to co-operate with little conflict. Emilio Mayorga notes a similar crossover situation that developed with the introduction of the Spanish-based CiM Madrid International Film Festival (No URL). According to Mayorga, the recently organised event is 'adding another festival to an already crowded European calendar' (2006). Yet, it is also quite possible that the addition of such an event will have little impact, as the organisers have already secured certain resources needed for operation from the Madrid Film Commission as well as from Madrid's municipal authorities. Thus, the festival essentially forms a niche in which the organisers must now prove their worth. Should they later wish to expand the event, however, and begin competing with other festivals, there will undoubtedly be an impact on the festival calendar.

Additional timing conflicts occur with respect to the date placement of film industry events such as the American Film Market, which also have the potential to limit a film festival's ability to attract resource provider participation. As SECOR Consulting explains, 'the most sought-after professionals have an embarrassment of choice and must be increasingly selective' (2004: 18). Film festival chronicler and theorist Marijke de Valck describes one such incident resulting from the 2004 repositioning of the Academy Awards® from its former late March position to its current late-February date which caused a chain reaction whereby

> the British Academy Film and Television Awards for film (the BAFTAs) were pushed forward a week to 15 February. This meant a near frontal collision with the Berlinale award ceremony on 14 February [...] If the Berlinale, however, could have moved a couple of days forward, the expected knock-on-effect would have affected the International Film Festival Rotterdam. (2007: 134)

The impact of these new dates was significantly less the next year, as the film festivals and their resource providers had been able to plan ahead and re-schedule accordingly. So, date shifts can be seen to have a tendency to only cause operational difficulties for a single cycle of operation, or at least until film festival organisers are able to address and amend the manner in which they deal with the situation.

Selecting a date because it is *seen* as important is a potentially flawed strategy because of the contrived nature of participation. The most effective means of applying this strategy is to consider where and when the resources required for operation are available. Lauri Tanner asked Mark Fishkin of any problems he may have had 'positioning the new Mill Valley Film Festival under the shadow of a major existing festival like the San Francisco International Film Festival?' (2009: 22). Fishkin replied that the organisers of Mill Valley 'were not trying to compete' and insisted there was no potential for threat as Mill Valley focused exclusively on a niche programming stream of Northern California Filmmakers (Ibid.). Such a technique of specifying the exact purpose of a film festival will be discussed in greater detail in Strategy Four.

Strategy Three: Location, Location, Location

Just as there is a time for a festival, so too, is there a place. The geographic location of a film festival is a widely-used means for motivating participation, especially the participation of those resource providers who are required to physically attend the event, such as audience members, filmmakers, media, etc. Marijke de Valck has discussed the planning that often occurs when deciding upon a film festival's geographical base:

> The physical location of the festival is very important for the festival's image of cultural difference and it is used in festival marketing strategies to compete with other film festivals. Location, the element most central to a festival's image,

is usually reflected in the name. By and large, festivals are named after the city where they take place. (2007: 137)

Fishkin makes a similar observation, suggesting that a connection exists between the uses of locations in the titling of film festival and its appeal:

Sometimes and even still today, when people are not aware of you, they automatically might think a festival in an urban area [which has] the name of a city means it's more important than a small town festival. But we know that's not really true. (Fishkin 2009c: 26)

For the most part, this strategy requires the film festival to be located in an area that is attractive or important in and of itself. For example, Jack Valenti, long-time president of the Motion Pictures Association of America, explains in Beauchamp and Béhar's book that there

is no question that part of the allure of Cannes is its location. If you started from scratch and said, "Where can we begin a festival that would attract an international audience year after year?" [...] I'm hard pressed to tell you a better place. (Beauchamp and Béhar 1992: 41)

A similar physical allure can be associated with the San Sebastian International Film Festival (www.sansebastianfestival.com), held in what is described as 'perhaps Spain's most beautiful town, with the country's highest standard of living, certainly its finest food' (Holland and Hopewell 2006). The motivation to attend is greatly increased among those potential participants eager to experience activities beyond those offered by the festival. The organisers of the Venice International Film Festival were once again most likely the first to implement this strategy, as de Valck explains:

One of the motivations for the establishment of the first reoccurring film festival in Venice in 1932 was tourism. The festival was carefully designed to attract as many visitors as possible to the city at a time when the tourist season was just coming to an end. (2007: 76)

Once again the overlap of this strategy of controlling an event's location with its timing is immediately apparent, and the economic benefits of the event on the community were instantaneous. Film festival scholar Ragan Rhyne reports that the addition of the film festival to Venice's tourist season calendar resulted in an increase of more than 25,000 people in its first year (2009: 11).

The tourism opportunities that film festivals bring to their communities are well-documented. Derek Elley explains that the organisation which set up the Swiss Locarno International Film Festival (www.pardo.ch/jahia/Jahia) started the festival 'just after World War II with tourism, not just film culture, on its mind' (1998: 113). Similarly, Beauchamp and Béhar note that the 'Cannes International Film Festival was heralded not only as a major film event, but as a general announcement to the world at large that the Riviera was again welcoming tourists' after World War II (1992: 44).

The use of a film festival for the purpose of promotion is termed by de Valck as 'City Marketing', and she explains that it has become 'a key concept in describing worldwide municipal strategies for the promotion of their cities since the 1980s' (2007: 75). It is important to note the level of community acceptance and monetary participation that is required from the population of a city where a film festival is situated. Macdonald calls this the 'infusion of cash that an off-season event can provide' and that motivates resort-style communities to host film festivals (1998: 39). Turan notes that the off-festival season population of Park City increases by over 20,000 people during Sundance (2002: 32). Such a volume of people attending the festival, and the city or town hosting the festival, requires co-ordination and communication between the festival organisers and the community members and services most likely to be directly influenced by it: hotels, public transport, police, hospitals and the like.

For those film festivals not located in a resort or known vacation spot, the geographic location of the event may still be used to their advantage. The placement of the Tribeca Film Festival in one of world's largest cities (New York City's population is estimated at just over 19 million) means organisers are able to facilitate 'a family festival that runs concurrently with the festival' (Amdur and Rooney 2004). With such a large population to draw on for its audiences, the Tribeca organisers are able to diversify their programming to include a wider demographic without compromising attendance at the core event, and even to engage in cross-promotion of the two.

The physical location of an event also enables its organisers to have greater access to resources that may otherwise be unavailable. Stephen Teo identifies the Busan, Hong Kong and the Singapore International Film Festivals as the 'three most important festivals in Asia because of their locations – all strategic hubs on the East Asian mainland stretching from the northeast to southeast – and because of their stated aim of promoting Asian cinema' (2009: 119). And critic Sheila Benson explains how the close proximity of the Mill Valley Film Festival to director George Lucas' Industrial Light & Magic studios, as well as to American Zoetrope (a.k.a Zoetrope Studios) has provided the organisers with 'access to the cache of technical talents who preferred the hills of Marin County to the hills of Hollywood' (1998: 148-9). A similar reference to proximity is made by the organisers of the Oakland-based Brainwash Movie Festival (www.brainwashm.com) in America. They state that both Robin Williams (who lives close by in Sea Cliff) and Showtime acquisitions agents have attended their Festival (Gore 2001: 263), thus offering incentives for wider participation.

Location can also promote a monopolistic or exclusive control over participation. That is, if a film festival's location is physically or culturally isolated it may represent the only interaction of its kind in an area. Thus, resource providers have no other option but to participate with the only organisation available that may be able to advance their own agendas. Gary Meyer, co-director of the Telluride Film Festival, comments on the success of the Palm Springs International Film Festival by saying that the local community is 'totally under-serviced [...] There are no art houses there, and none of the theatres show anything but the very biggest of art films, and usually quite late' (Meyer 2009: 76). By contrast, Simon Field explains that 'Paris would be an impossible place to have a festival, because there are films everywhere already [...] festivals should be in anonymous cities with few distractions' (Field 2009: 71). This situation is confirmed by de Valck, for whom one of the reasons that Paris was not chosen as the original location of the Cannes International Film Festival is that

> If it had been located in Paris it would have had a much harder time of distinguishing itself from the ample supply of other cultural activities in Paris. In short, the location on the Riviera contributed to its exclusivity and appeal. (2007: 115)

Some film festivals only accept entries from local suppliers, such as the American Northwest Film & Video Festival (www.nwfilm.org), which limits its programming to films produced by 'artists residing in Oregon, Washington, Idaho, Montana, Alaska and British Colombia' (Gore 2001: 311). The strategy of restricting from where certain resources originate, may serve to elevate the film festival's stature as it grows to represent the authority of that particular source of films in that geographic location.

There are instances, too, in which the geographic location actually works to the detriment of a festival. In 2006, organisers of the Busan International Film Festival received lower numbers of attendees due to a recent bomb test in North Korea (Frater 2006). The challenges associated with geographical positioning are often circumstantial and fluid, so if North Korea were to be viewed as less of a danger zone, the challenges arising from Busan's geographical location would decrease proportionally.

Regardless of the setting of any film festival there are always advantages afforded by the location and one should never underestimate the benefits of being close to someone or something. Having access to money, goods, in-kind services and people, and without the need to travel vast distances, not only saves time and money for a festival organiser, but can also set in motion a snowballing local effect that can prove the difference in sustaining an event during difficult economic times.

Strategy Four: Have an Identifiable Function

Why another film festival? This strategy consists of providing a recognisable purpose or intent for a film festival through an overt means – a mission statement, expressed goals or objectives, etc. – so as to clearly communicate the event's capacity for operation. Having an identifiable function separates a festival from the herd. Whether providing a platform for films based entirely on the fact that they feature insects, or for more politically-charged and socially redeeming reasons, film festivals with specific goals can take advantage of such a focus in their organisation. For example, when the America-based Human Rights Watch International Film Festival (ff.hrw.org) identifies itself as a 'showcase for films related to human rights subject matter [in the form of] documentary, fiction and animation of any length' (Gaydos 1998: 97), such a description at once gives the film festival a *raison d'être* and a recognisable form. The identified function of a film festival can be seen to effectively frame a participant's understanding of the boundaries of the event prior to their interaction. Explicitly stated examples of identifiable functions include: the French Festival du Court Métrage en Plein Air de Grenoble (Open Air Festival of Short Film in Grenoble) (festivalgrenoble.ifrance.com), which describes its programming as including 'new and old talents, with both indoor and open-air screenings' (Gaydos 1998: 106), the Internet-based Charged 60-Second Film Festival (www.chargedfilmfestival.com / broken URL) with a competition 'dedicated to films and videos of one minute or less' (Gore 2001: 264), and the U.S.-based Tech TV's Cam Film Festival (no URL), which is 'designed to teach people how to use their new digital cameras and home editing equipment' (2001: 331).

An identifiable function serves to dispel any potential ambiguity as to the exact role of the event and enables potential participants to assess for themselves the specific benefits they may receive from interaction. This aspect of resource provider self-assessment is important given the exposure and publicity film festivals generally receive, and it enables film festival organisers to take advantage of potential participants beyond the immediate geographical area. So, the Cucalorus Film Festival (www. cucalorus.org) states that its goal is 'to bring independent film culture and awareness to Wilmington [North Carolina]. We strive to display deserving work, creating a noncompetitive showcase of films spawned from all budgets, by filmmakers of all backgrounds' (Gore 2001: 270). This is a pretty explicit statement by the festival organisers that not only identifies the function of the film festival, but also addresses what type of filmmakers should consider participating, thus enabling the organisers to raise awareness of the event without having contact with resource providers.

The strategy of providing a festival with an identifiable function has arisen from the legalities involved in operating formal organisations. For scholar and non-profit specialist Carl Milofsky, formal organisations are 'social systems that are legally constituted to achieve goals' (1988: 10). Many organisations often do not achieve these goals, but through the very process of goal-setting are able to structure 'explicit membership boundaries, articulating a decision-making structure and hierarchy of power, and defining the participants' activities' (Ibid.).

The construction of such membership boundaries and defining of activities helps to encourage participation by framing the parameters of interaction and providing a basis for understanding what involvement may entail. Fishkin explains how the organisers of the Mill Valley Film Festival were able to structure interaction around the phrase 'a celebration of the art of film' noting how organisers 'intentionally wanted an atmosphere that was <u>not</u> competitive, that people could come here and celebrate' (Fishkin 2009c: 26, emphasis in original). The purpose of creating a specific 'atmosphere' is strategic in that it directly appeals to the expectations of the participants: people who have never been to a film festival before may attend an event expecting it to operate in a manner similar to a commercial theatre screening, and thereby assess the event according to an incorrect frame of reference, potentially jeopardising their future interaction. The use of such terms as 'celebration' and 'art of film', serves to signpost the nature of the event, and thus (hopefully) condition any preconceived notions of the film festival that potential participants may have. Even if potential participants do not fully understand what the terms mean, the strategy of employing an identifiable function can alter their expectations enough to promote a more open frame of mind. Gail Silva, former director of the Film Arts Foundation, comments on a festival she organised:

> We just wanted to keep the word 'independent' visible within all the stuff we did, but we knew that most people didn't know what the words 'independent film and video' meant, didn't understand its context [...] we knew what we had to sell were the ideas of the pieces. (Silva 2009: 70; emphasis in original)

An identifiable function can also serve as a rallying point for specific interest groups. For example, the U.S.-based Hi Mom! Film Festival (www.himomfilmfestival.org) describes itself as 'a festival for filmmakers with big ideas and little bank accounts' (Gore 2001: 284). Similarly, Slamdance's catch cry of 'for filmmakers, by filmmakers' is an overt display of the film festival's purported ideological alignment. Acknowledging that a festival has a preference for a particular type of participant also enables organisers to effectively remove any ambiguity as to who should participate in their film festival. For example, organisers of the Dances with Films (www.danceswithfilms.com) in California announced that films submitted into the film festival had 'no "known" directors, actors or producers' (Gore 2001: 271). This type of boundary-setting is an important time saver: organisers can avoid expending time and energy fostering interactions with resource providers who do not fit the ideological frame of the festival, efficiently preventing the wrong participants from attending.

The 'purpose or the mission of the festival' is, from a film critic's point of view at least, the first aspect festival organisers need to convey (Fox 2009: 146). This needs to be done so that the critic or journalist is able to first identify the event as a story, and then decide if the festival is worth attending. By discouraging unsuitable participants from interacting, film festival organisers avoid unnecessary or misdirected scrutiny of the event that could result in the future non-participation of particular resource providers due to previous bad experiences they may have had or heard about. One foreseeable danger of this strategy is the possible alienation of the festival due to an overly-niche appeal. So, as journalist Craig Alexander explains, the World's Worst Movies Festival (no URL) was unable to 'sustain [the] interest' of members of its Ottawan community base because of the limited appeal of its programming over time (1997). Organisers of events such as the Illinois-based Freaky Film Festival (no URL) which charged itself with an 'annual mission' of providing 'our audience with diverse and unpredictable programs' (Gore 2001: 280) were likely to encounter a similar lack of support should their programmes become too diverse or unpredictable.

Film festival organisers are also likely to encounter difficulties if they do not remain faithful to or operate according to their identified function. The perceived legitimacy of an event's operations can hang on it. Cathy Hope relates one such legitimacy problem encountered during the early operation of the Sydney and Melbourne International Film Festivals. She explains how the festivals nearly compromised their 'cultural legitimacy' as 'exhibitors of non-mainstream "quality" cinema' (2004: 1) because the programming of certain films gave the events the appearance of being 'promotion devices for the commercial trade' (2004:196).

For Sambolgo Bangré, many film festivals promote the same objectives: 'to distribute and promote films; to enable film-makers, critics, the public and producers to meet; to offer an opportunity to get to know the realities of different film-makers and of their countries'. Still, these 'noble objectives' may mask other 'ambitions' (1996: 158). Perhaps the most well-known example of ulterior motives comes once again with the Venice International Film Festival and its use by Mussolini to promote Fascist political ideas (Rooney 1998: 121). Scholar Marla Stone relates how at 'its 1932 inauguration, the film festival made a splash, [by] projecting forty films from nine nations' (2002: 294), but that despite this show of egalitarianism, the ambitions of the festival's Fascist organisers soon became evident. By 1935 the 'political overtones were clear' and scepticism as to the validity of the original goal of the festival in 'recognizing filmmaking as art' became palpable (Beauchamp and Béhar 1992: 43). An obvious bias in the selection of films for awards was apparent when films from Nazi Germany won the Best Foreign Film awards in 1937 and 1938 (Stone 2002: 296). The perceived illegitimacy of the event led to a split between the Axis and Allied nations, resulting in the formation of the Cannes International Film Festival in 1939. In 1940, the official title of the Venice festival was changed to underline that political allegiance which had been so obvious to many: it became the Manifestazione Cinematografica Italo-Germanica – the Italian-German Film Festival (Ibid.). The transition from 'recognizing filmmaking as art' to propaganda machine for German and Italian Fascist ideals is a predictable result given the make-up of the festival's primary resource providers. That is, since the Fascist government was the underwriter of the film festival, it became inevitable that the latter would reflect the ideology of the former.

Strategy Five: Encourage Legitimizing Affiliations

A legitimizing affiliation consists of a film festival's partnership or connection with another organisation, business or individual, which gives the film festival a level of credibility that in turn positively influences the motivation of other potential participants. Such an affiliation may be internal to the festival organisation, as when the founder of the film festival is a recognised figure, as in the case with Robert De Niro and the Tribeca Film Festival, or it may be external in the sense that it derives from such an interaction as the corporate sponsorship of an event.

This strategy is based on the idea that previous participation validates future operation. It differs from the strategy of co-operative alliances in that each legitimizing affiliation is focused on enhancing the image of the film festival and not necessarily on the contribution of physical resources to the actual operation of the event. In other words, through the extant or previous participation of particular people or groups, film festival organisers are able to prove to potential resource providers that their event is a viable Open System; a system that is displaying negative entropy. This strategy of legitimizing affiliations, as its name suggests, frames participation so as to portray the festival as having an inherent organisational legitimacy due to its interaction with worthy and important participants. For example, Claude Jarman, former executive director of the San Francisco International Film Festival, describes how support from the Mayor of San Francisco gave the event organisers a 'stamp of authenticity' (Jarman 2009: 108).

The efficacy of such stamps of authenticity is acknowledged by Biskind who describes how organisers of Sundance 'clung' to director Steven Soderbergh following the success of his film *Sex, Lies, and Videotape* (U.S., 1989), using him as a 'poster boy for the festival' (2004: 83). The connection between Sundance and Soderbergh can be seen to be intended to manipulate potential participants by drawing a link between the success of the director and his interaction or affiliation with the event. The New York Expo of Short Film and Video (www.stockshotstudio.com/nyexpo/history.html) was another film festival that explicitly employed this strategy when claiming its event as one 'of the first festivals to recognize the talents of Spike Lee, George Lucas and Martha Coolidge' (Gore 2001: 308). To combat the tyranny of distance, early Australian film festivals and Australian distributors established strategic links along these lines in order to 'encourage overseas distributors to give the Festivals more, and better, films' (Hope 2004: 75). This encouragement stemmed from the belief that affiliations with the Australian distributors would legitimise the festivals and lead to a greater probability of international films receiving distribution.

The use of 'stamps of approval', of 'poster boys' and of film industry connections, ultimately serves to raise the perceived value of an event and thereby affords the organisers a great opportunity to motivate potential participants. Paul DiMaggio and Walter Powell are social theorists who discuss aspects of organisational prestige in their examination of what is known as institutional isomorphism and the collective rationality found in organisational fields. According to them a 'status competition' exists within certain organisational fields that results in a general pattern in which 'organizational prestige and resources are key elements in attracting professionals' (1988: 87). Such 'status competition' can be readily observed in the milieu of film festivals which Robert Koehler describes as a 'never-ending race between festivals to score points' over each other (2009: 81).

Legitimizing affiliation is also a strategy congruent with the findings of organisational theorists Joseph Galaskiewicz and Barbara Rauschenbach, for whom it is common for a cultural organisation to be seen as 'striving to enhance its prestige through association with the more influential corporations' (1988: 132). This enhancement of prestige often occurs with the patronage of film festivals by such individuals as well-known and respected directors, critics, actors, artists, etc., whose participation is often seen as a headlining event. For example, Harris mentions in a *Variety On-line* article, subtitled 'Talent Flock to Latest Edition of SXSW Fest', that the number of 'celebs who braved the weather included Crispin Glover, Christina Ricci, Adam Goldberg and Janine Turner' (2004b). Beauchamp and Béhar remember how at the 1949 Cannes Film Festival 'Errol Flynn, Rita Hayworth, Tyrone Power, Yves Montand and Pablo Picasso began the tradition of walking up the red-carpeted Palais steps' (1992: 131).

Marshalling the 'glamour and fantasy of Hollywood' (Stone 2002: 295) has been used as a method of displaying a film festival's legitimacy since the inaugural Venice International Film Festival. Yet, the strategy of employing legitimizing affiliations does not require a film festival to always and actually attain the participation of the most valued individuals or organisations. Rather, as discussed by Galaskiewicz and Rauschenbach, it is sometimes enough for an organisation to 'receive corporate support – it is not necessary to link up with the more influential corporations in town' (1988: 133) in order to reap the benefits of affiliation.

Film festival organisers can utilise any contacts and partnerships they deem to be capable of raising the organisational legitimacy in their event. Tanner stresses the importance of evaluating and promoting the 'current and potential endorsers/supporters/sponsors, including individuals, organizations and businesses; plus information on any collaborative relationships that might currently exist with other groups or companies which would potentially relate to this project [film festival]' (2009: 168). Sometimes the best resources are the people you are already in contact with.

Affiliations can be further categorised into five distinct subgroups: organisers, organisations, patrons/official guests (including actors, directors and other celebrities), boards of directors and sponsors. The purpose of such delineation is to indicate the unique importation-based advantages each group presents to film festival organisers. Film festival organisers may utilise any number or combination of groups when employing this strategy, and no one particular group presents itself as the best possible option under all conditions.

Organiser-based affiliation. Organisers are those individuals who are internal to the film festival organisation: programmer, programme manager or festival director. These individuals contribute to the overall prestige of an event by their reputation among and relationship with their resource providers. These are individuals who, in the modern culture of film festivals, have become recognisable in the contemporary festival scene, which has become to some extent 'The Age of Festival Directors' (de Valck 2007: 191). For example, Anne Mackenzie, former co-ordinator of the Canada-based Women and Film International Festival was hired as the first programme manager of the Toronto International Film Festival because she had experience facilitating a film festival previously in Toronto. She could utilise her contacts to help establish a reputation for her new employer more quickly than if the event organisers had hired an individual with no known qualities in that area (Johnson 2000). Clearly then, Mackenzie's involvement could be viewed as offering a strategic advantage for the Toronto International Film Festival.

An organiser is able to contribute strategically to the importation of resources when they are able to effectively manipulate the interpersonal nature of their work. In a manner similar to successful corporate movers and shakers, efficacious film festival organisers possess a particular skill set that enables them to be fruitful when interacting with resource providers. So, when Murray 'Dusty' Cohl, co-founder of the Toronto International Film Festival, is noted as seeming 'to have a gift for meeting all the journalists' while attending Cannes, this only serves to promote the inauguration of his own event later that year (Johnson 2000: 24). Hope comments on the effectiveness of Erwin Rado, festival director of the Melbourne International Film Festival from 1954 to 1979 (2004: 64), and of David Stratton, festival director of the Sydney Film Festival from 1966 to 1983 (2004: 141), when the two conducted their individual visits to international distributors on behalf of their respective Australian festivals. This is a specialised business and needs specialised people. Gilmore puts the lie to the common misconception of film festivals 'as things that anybody can do, all you need to know is a little bit about movies', by advocating for the selection of a film festival organiser to be seen as on a par with the selection of the co-ordinator of 'an arts organization, a museum, or a symphony' (Gilmore 2009: 136).

The relationships that form between film festival organisers and their various resource providers give some film festivals undeniable advantages in their resource importation. The international sales director of France's Wild Bunch is in contact with the organisers of both Cannes and Venice all year round (Peranson 2009), and the fact that the current festival director of Cannes, Thierry Frémaux, previously worked as that festival's artistic director (Elley and Hopewell 2007), or that Marco Müller served as the festival director of Locarno, Rotterdam and Pesaro before being hired by Venice in 2004 (Vivarelli 2004; de La Fuente 2004) can be no mere coincidence. Soon after Müller took up his position at Venice, he hired Elenora Granata to be the event's representative in the United States, citing her 'rare combination of experience and exuberance that the festival will fully benefit from. Her impressive industry relationship along with her artistic sensibility fit perfectly with our vision of the festival's future' (de La Fuente 2003). That it took Palm Springs International Film Festival 'several years to recover' when director Darryl Macdonald resigned (Gaydos 1998: 47) is proof positive of the importance of particular organisers to particular events.

The founders of the Zurich Film Festival include a programme manager who is a 'popular character actor in films and television', and a marketing manager who is a 'well-known model' (Grey 2006); the German Hof International Film Festival (www.hofer-filmtage.de) is noted for being under the directorship of 'one of the most respected German film enthusiasts, Heinz Badewits' (Cowie 2003: 375); Spain's Tudela First Film Festival is touted as being 'run by popular journalist Luis Alegre' (2003: 419); and the prestige of the U.S.-based Roger Ebert's Overlooked Film Festival (Ebertfest) (www.ebertfest.com), which is programmed and hosted by the prominent film critic himself, is similarly elevated by such an affiliation (Gore 2001: 319).

It is important to note that not all organiser-based affiliations are beneficial to film festival operation, which provides further testament to the importance of such affiliations. Kong Rithdee explains how the Thailand government contracted a Los Angeles-based company, Film Festival Management Inc., to facilitate the Bangkok International Film Festival from 2003 to 2006 by trading on that company's access to the 'glitz and glamour' of celebrities and their specialisation in 'special gala events' (2009: 128). According to Kong, the American organisers contributed to 'one of the most shocking infamies in the history of international film festivals' (2009: 122) in that they actually had 'little experience in managing a film festival' (2009: 124) and ended up spending 100 times more than had been originally budgeted. To further sour the situation, the owners of Film Festival Management were later found guilty of bribing a high-ranking official in the Thai government (2009: 122).

Another potentially problematic situation is identified by film critic Stephen Teo who explains that the 'same people who ran SIFF [Singapore International Film Festival] (www.siff.sg) at its inception twenty years ago are still running it today – a sign that the organisation is sorely in need of generational change' (2009: 117). A similar lack of staff turnover was attributed with influencing the performance level of the Experimental Film Festival in New York. Co-founder of the festival, Sarah Schulman, bemoaned the fact that she and her colleagues 'didn't go to fancy schools', which 'hurt the festival because we didn't have the connections, we didn't know all the fancy people' (Gamson 1996: 250). The organisers decided to 'pass the torch' to two younger, ethnic filmmakers 'whose work the founders admired' (249), and whose educational backgrounds included study at Harvard University and New York University's Studio Art and Cinema Studies Program. Gamson identifies two advantages of this organisational turnover using terminology that is now familiar within the context of this monograph and serves to reinforce the identification of film festivals as Open Systems whose existence relies on the successful importation of and transformation of resources to promote negative entropy:

> First, it furnished the festival with new human resources, while promising to transform it into an organization more directly connected to and more adequately serving communities of color. Second, it provided the festival with new potential survival resources, not in the form of direct economic support [...] but in the form of increased cultural and social capital (Ibid.)

Organisation-based affiliation. Organisation-based affiliation takes place for those film festivals that originate from an already existing entity, such as a film society or arts festival. The Austin, Texas-based South by Southwest Film Festival (sxsw.com/film) was formed as part of an already operating, highly successful event presenting a Music and Media Conference (Gore 2001), which began in 1987; the film festival was officially added in 1994. Additional examples of film festivals that stemmed from pre-existing organisations include: the Venice International Film Festival (via the Venice Biennale) (Stone 2002; de Valck 2007; Beauchamp and Béhar 1992), the London Film Festival (via the British Film Institute) (Elley 1998) and the Freedom Film Festival (via the American Cinema Foundation) (www.cinemafoundation.com) in the U.S. (Gore 2001).

There are several advantages to having a film festival grow from an already functional event, not least of which is that the host organisation offers the film festival the legitimizing presence of a proven operational infrastructure. Film festival organisers are likely to benefit from previously secured resource channels that have been developed by the presenting organisation. *Cineaste* assistant editor, Rahul Hamid, explains how the Film Society of the Lincoln Center completely underwrote the New York Film Festival for its first years of operation through a New Projects Fund (2009: 72). This secured source of funding enabled the film festival organisers to devote their undivided attention to more central aspects of the event such as programming and audience building. Without this advantage it is likely that the New York Film Festival organisers would have experienced what Geoffrey Gilmore calls the 'steal from Peter to pay Paul' scenario that afflicts many film festivals at some time (Gilmore 2009: 135).

Film festival organisers are continually devising and developing new funding streams in the form of, for example, fundraising events such as preview screenings, so as to establish an economic base. But these activities can be distracting and the film festival organiser may sometimes neglect to reinvest enough into the film festival itself, thus leaving it 'to scratch and survive in a (bare-bones) budget operation' (Gilmore 2009: 135). Because there are always areas of operation that are continually veering towards entropy through resource depletion, such a situation diminishes the capabilities of the film festival organisers to develop the film festival to its full potential.

Organisation-based affiliations can protect film festivals from the forces of entropy that would otherwise see the operation of an individually functioning event grind to a halt. The Vancouver International Film Festival, for example, is organised under the Greater Vancouver International Film Festival Society (SECOR 2004). As part of this larger society, festival organisers are able to access the Vancouver International Film Center, which contains 'state-of-the-art projection and sound equipment', for their festival screenings (Vancouver International Film Centre 2008), thus reducing the financially-driven entropy that occurs through operation.

A host organisation can also provide a film festival with access to an established social network, which can include necessities as diverse as e-mail addresses or an audience base. An example of the latter comes, once again, with the Greater Vancouver International Film Festival Society, which has 41,000 members (SECOR 2004) and is involved in co-operative alliances with other community organisations. This access enables the festival to implement more comprehensive aspects of interaction, such as film education, as opposed to just trying to secure audience participation. The result of this established social network provides relief from participation-driven entropy and ensures that the festival overcomes those attendance problems which may hinder the operation of other independent events.

Patrons/official guests-based affiliation. An affiliation with patrons and official guests provides legitimacy to an event through the very cachet of their positions as people of social or industry importance. Patrons and official guests generally serve both functions, the usual difference being the more transient nature of the latter's participation: patrons are individuals who are affiliated with a film festival on an ongoing basis, while official guests may change from event to event and generally only remain at the film festival for a short period. The 'typical guest' at the Venice International Film Festival, for example, only attends the film festival for three out of the 11 days of the event (de Valck 2007: 132).

Both patrons and official guests are courted by the festival because of the esteem in which they are held in fields beyond that of the film festival itself, and although some individuals' vocations may be in politics, music, sports, etc., the majority of people affiliated with film festivals in this way are from the film industry. As a general rule, the more accomplished or important the patron or guest – an Academy Award® winning director is usually more desirable than a stuntman – the more valuable the affiliation is to the film festival.

For the most part patrons are not required to be involved in the operation of the film festival, but serve only in an ambassadorial role. Official guests, on the other hand, may play a more active role in the operation of the event by participating as jury members, by hosting master classes or by introducing films, etc. The importation-based advantages of having such individuals affiliated with the festival are twofold. First, the attendance of a celebrity or respected filmmaker can help to 'rarify' the event. That is, participants such as audience members, reporters and film critics, are more likely to attend an event if it presents a unique, exclusive experience. According to Fox, a film review will rarely be on the front page of an entertainment section, or a Sunday section, but an interview will be. So just having a filmmaker come to the festival means [film festival organisers] have a chance for wider exposure. (Fox 2009: 146)

Second, the affiliation of known individuals can improve the perceived validity of the film festival and strengthen its identifiable function, thus influencing the motivation for a resource provider to participate. Actor Leonardo DiCaprio, for example, is the patron of the online Leofest, which positions itself as a potential platform for aspiring filmmakers. This identifiable function is given additional legitimacy by a personal message from the patron himself: 'I've been around artists my entire life. Breaking through – when you are just starting out – can seem impossible [...] this festival strives to offer a level playing field on which anyone who wishes may play' (DiCaprio 1999). Similarly, the participation of Catherine Breillat, Ridley Scott and a 'host of Oscar® winners', at the Berlin Talent Campus in 2005 (Barraclough 2004), served to motivate aspiring film industry professionals to apply for one of the 500 available positions.

A similar legitimisation is observable in the participation of Steven Spielberg, George Lucas and Francis Ford Coppola at the 2004 French-based Deauville American Film Festival (www.festival-deauville.com), which is dedicated to screening 'yesterday's, today's and tomorrow's' American Cinema (Deauville 2012). The attendance of three of Hollywood's most iconic directors not only validated this stated function, but also 'provided a major boost to the financially pinched fest' (James and Nesselson 2004).

Additionally, some film festivals elect to present awards and tributes named after particular individuals of significant stature. Actor Antonio Banderas received 'a Gabi Lifetime Achievement award' at the 10th edition of the Los Angeles Latino International Film Festival (latinofilm.org/festival) (de La Fuente 2006), for example. The 'Gabi' is named after influential Mexican cinematographer Gabriel Figueroa and is an award that not only serves to legitimise the film festival through this very affiliation, but also attracts respected guests, such as Banderas, who are then seen to be honoured to receive an award with such a prestigious name attached. A similar technique is employed by Macedonia's Manaki Brothers' International Cinematographers Film Festival (www.manaki.com.mk), which, rather than presenting an award in an individual's name is actually named 'after the first Balkan cameraman' (Gaydos 1998: 140). Such a strategy works as a form of coding, attracting those individuals who are familiar with this particular aspect of film production and who are likely to benefit most from participation.

The attendance of official guests at a film festival is not always to the benefit of the event. Many times celebrities attend film festivals merely as part of contractual agreements with a film distributor which is, in turn, using the publicity generated at the event to raise public awareness of its film. Dana Harris and Brendan Kelly (2004) noted how an array of 'celebrities have obliged their studios' intentions' by attending the Toronto International Film Festival (2004), and Harris described how the rapper Ludacris managed to abide by 'the letter of the law' in his contract with William Morris Agency by spending a total of exactly '90 seconds' promoting the 2005 film *Hustle & Flow* (Craig Brewer, U.S., 2005) at the Sundance Film Festival's official post-screening party (2005).

In cases such as this, where the guest is not procured through personal contacts, but rather arranged through business means, the festival can risk exposure to unforeseen costs in terms of both social and economic capital. Not all guests' behaviour can be predicted. This is exemplified by actor Doris Day and her husband being given use of a car courtesy of the French Government during their visit to the Cannes Film Festival, which they promptly drove to Italy at their host's expense (Beauchamp and Béhar 1992, 170). A similar social and economic *faux pas* was committed at Cannes by visiting festival guest Robert Mitchum who decided to take a 'bath in champagne', sparking a *'crise diplomatique'* when he checked out of the hotel and left the film festival to cover the cost of his unorthodox and bubbly ablutions (Beauchamp and Béhar 1992, 170).

Film festival organisers must also be wary of the baggage certain guests can bring as part of their reputation; their attendance may not always produce the desired effect among the other participants and just as reflected glory can be an outcome of fraternising with the stars, so too can guilt by association. Such was the case for the unfortunate Palm Springs International Film Festival when it presented Sylvester Stallone with a lifetime achievement award. According to Gaydos, the action star's 'decidedly mixed body of work created a critical backlash both in and out of the fest[ival]'s infrastructure that threatened to diminish the fest's very substantial progress over the past decade in planning and programming' (1998c: 46).

Board of directors-based affiliation. The board of directors is that body of individuals internal to the film festival structure whose role is generally characterised by their involvement in the planning and offering of advice/guidance to the event's physical operator, the film festival director. This understanding is congruent with the description of a festival's organisational structure as presented by SECOR Consulting.

They note that the function of Canadian board members is important for fundraising and supervision, but that, in general, the members of film festival boards are 'not involved in operational or programming decisions, or in event organization, etc. However, any major change of direction or positioning (e.g. change of dates) must be submitted to and ratified by the board' (2004: 21). There are instances in which the board members of a film festival also act as its physical facilitators. Fishkin explains how the Mill Valley Film Festival, when it first commenced operation, had only three board members and that the operations-based responsibilities were shared between them according to their employment backgrounds (Fishkin 2009a). The adoption of a dual role for personnel can be seen to streamline the operational process, however, as Galaskiewicz and Rauschenbach explain, the more sources of decisional input there are, 'the less influence any one of them is likely to have' (1988: 121). Film festivals that boast numerous board members – Toronto has 33, Cannes 28 and Sundance 25 (SECOR 2004) – may not be able to respond efficiently to dramatic changes in the film festival environment due to bureaucratic delays, e.g. holding a meeting in which a quorum is present, reaching a consensus, etc.

Like hiring a well-known festival director, the incorporation of reputable board members can also serve to legitimise the operation of an event; or, as Galaskiewicz and Rauschenbach note, 'cultural organizations may put executives of very influential companies on their board to lead others to believe that they are very prestigious' (1988: 120). Board members are generally recruited from the film industry and from the business sector; SECOR Consulting explains that board members of the Vancouver International Film Festival are 'drawn from the local film and business communities and British Columbia public organizations' (2004: 25).

The decision to choose board members from specific backgrounds or vocations is a strategy which can give a film festival greater access to a particular resource provider. Ron Henderson explains that it is important for film festivals to have individuals on the board who can 'open other doors for you [the festival director] in the community' (Henderson 2009: 126). Thus, when Hope notes that the committee of the Melbourne International Film Festival was 'primarily made up of film culture figures', while that of the Sydney Film Festival 'contained many representatives from the film industry' (2004: 59), it can be deduced that the make-up of each board was indicative of that particular area upon which each festival was most likely to call for resources.

Additional, importation-based benefits to be gained through board of directors-based affiliations include access to social networks for the purpose of fundraising (SECOR 2004: 23) and, according to founder and director of the Cinequest San Jose Film Festival in California (www. cinequest.org), Halfdan Hussey, the provision of 'cash contacts all of the year' (Hussey 2009: 138). Most board members understand that their membership translates into financial or in-kind support of the festival and, as Galaskiewicz and Rauschenbach argue, festivals which operate on a non-profit basis

> will often indicate to their board members that they are expected to 'hit up' their employer for a corporate contribution [...] because companies should be more responsive to the request which an employee makes on behalf of a nonprofit than to the request of a stranger. (1988: 123)

The strategic use of board member affiliation is not without its problems, though. In fact, the resignation of Darryl Macdonald from Palm Springs International Film Festival was the result of a conflict between the director and the board members regarding the festival's artistic direction (Dawes 1993). Most board members 'usually know little about cinema' (Koehler 2009: 82), so perceptions of their interference in such decisions as an event's artistic direction can bring about internal clashes and haggling that can adversely influence the importation of resources. Alan Franey, the executive director of the Vancouver International Film Festival, discusses the intricacies of this situation:

> I think a Board should know when to hire a competent person, and then let that person do it, and leave them alone [...] I get countless manuals on arts administration, and I have yet to see one that would echo my own sentiment – which is run it like a business, not an arts organization. There are far more events that have been screwed up by the good intentions of their Board than helped. (Franey 2009: 31)

Halfdan Hussey shrewdly advises that when constructing a board of directors it is important to find people

> who are very effective at what they do but are also very busy, because they'll want to help you quickly and not be involved in taking control of the organization and getting their nose into things like the daily operations. (Hussey 2009: 138)

Sponsor-based affiliations. Sponsors are organisations, funding bodies, institutions or individuals, that contribute to the financial security of a film festival, for philanthropic or for business reasons, through the provision of monetary contributions, be they cash or in-kind. Sponsorship 'accounts for a very large portion of most festivals' revenues. Beyond being a source of income, sponsorship testifies to an event's prestige and impact by allowing major companies to become partners' (SECOR 2004: 48). The total amount of sponsorship, and the degree to which sponsorship interaction occurs, is particular to each film festival, and although the details are usually governed by commercial-in-confidence clauses, organisers may be able to make the existence of some partnerships more overt in order to increase the potential for further participant involvement.

According to Paul DiMaggio and Walter Powell, 'government recognition of key firms or organizations through the grant or contract process may give these organizations legitimacy and visibility' (1988: 86). Thus, contracted visibility agreements, in the form of naming rights, logo placement and product giveaways, between film festivals and their sponsors, may be more readily agreed upon, as the image of these participants contributes to the identifiable legitimacy of the event. Michael Lumpkin explains how an affiliation between the German Goethe-Institut and the San Francisco International Lesbian and Gay Film Festival gave the event 'credibility' (Lumpkin 2009: 130). Similarly, Tony Rayns notes that the involvement of the Busan City Council in the Busan International Film Festival positively influenced the acceptance of the event among other resource providers: as 'soon as the City Council came on board, the sponsorship followed' (Rayns 2009: 88). When the Hong Kong International Film Festival lost its major sponsor, Cathay-Pacific Airlines, organisers continued 'staging glitzy events' that had 'the effect of concealing any sense of crisis or financial hardship from the public' (Teo 2009: 115). This 'staging' of an event appears to have been a conscious decision by the organisers to prevent any possible de-motivation or further loss of participants and their accompanying resource input due to a perceived legitimacy problem.

Though sponsorship may be integral to the operation of a film festival, it also represents one of the greatest threats. Sponsors naturally desire that a festival functions to accommodate their own ideas and purposes and so there is always the risk of communicating mixed or conflicting messages about the festival's identifiable function: is it a festival, or an elaborate piece of advertising? For example, Harris describes the Sundance Film Festival has having 'fallen victim to relentless celebrity coverage and the bottomless deep pockets of corporate sponsorship' (2005). She observes a growing restlessness between the film festival organisers who understand that the event 'couldn't exist without its own raft of corporate sponsors', but still wonders how a dog food company

Alex Fischer

managed to become associated with the celebration of independent films (Ibid.). Such affiliations provide easy points of attack for critics such as Koehler, who considers the event 'a horror show for cinema: a place where more bad films can be seen under awful viewing conditions than any other festival' (2009: 84).

Even for social theorists such as Galaskiewicz and Rauschenbach the 'understanding of the relationship between the business donor and the cultural organisation is still incomplete at best' (1988: 119). Film festival operation only serves to confirm this and is rife with sponsorship complexities that may have detrimental effects on resource importation. For Simon Field, the focus of sponsorship is often directed towards an association with 'glamorous people' rather than at the festival itself, and he sees this as a chief reason why 'people who are not film-involved want a festival' (Field 2009: 59).

To further complicate matters 'corporations may make cash contributions in exchange for a position on the board of directors and shared control over the cultural organization' (Galaskiewicz & Rauschenbach 1988: 119). In such cases the administrative power of a particular board member may override the decisions of other board members and sponsors, thus elevating the potential for internal conflict. The Tourism Authority of Thailand once identified the Bangkok International Film Festival as having the potential to become one of that city's 'flagship spectacles in its annual tourism calendar'. Consequently, the government organisation effectively high-jacked the event from the original sponsors, removing them and re-designating the dates of the film festival to align with a month devoid of any other agency activity (Kong Rithdee 2009: 128).

The external control that is commonly expected by sponsors as a by-product of their sponsorship is an aspect of Open System operation that can complicate matters for many film festival organisers. Ron Henderson provides further insight into this give-and-take aspect of participation by advising film festival organisers to ask themselves the following question:

> How much do you give up in order to get money [...] In those kinds of relationships, you need to look exactly at what it is they want, and what you're going to have to give up and whether you can live with that or not. (Henderson 2009: 123)

Strategy Six: Offer Participation-based Incentives

The strategy of offering participation-based incentives utilises the gratification that drives social system interaction in order to manipulate resource providers by targeting and promoting those perceived benefits of interaction that are of greatest value to them and to the festival. So, when identifying '10 Important Factors to Consider when Applying to Festivals' for prospective participants, Gore (2001: 26-8) found that the festival's 'prestige', ranked first, above both its 'location' (identified as fifth) and the 'fun' to be expected (listed as 10th) by visitors. Such incentives, as well as their inherent value to a resource provider, are dependent on a number of circumstances, including:

1) The reason for participating – a distributor, celebrity, or film critic may attend a film festival as part of their job, while a member of the general public usually attends for reasons of entertainment or education.

2) The need for participation – Beauchamp and Béhar describe a 'must attend' relationship that exists between the Cannes Film Festival and the film industry, and liken the festival to 'an international summit, the annual convention of all those who have anything to do with filmmaking. It has become the annual crossroads for the world's film industry and now almost demands participation' (1992: 23).

3) The benefits of participation – SECOR Consulting illustrates that government agencies aim to become involved in film festivals that are seen to have 'significant (direct and indirect) economical impact, as well as important social and cultural benefits' (2004: 5). Through their support, these agencies may achieve recognition thereby providing 'ideal leverage for achieving cultural objectives' (Ibid.).

This *quid pro quo* strategy is explained by Galaskiewicz and Rauschenbach in explicit Open System terms, when they note that

> the acquisition of scarce resources is of primary importance to organizations. Although organizations may prefer to remain autonomous, as open systems they need to secure resources from actors in their environment and will engage in exchange transactions to do so. (1988: 120)

The use of participation-based incentives is a means of ensuring that a film festival will have the best opportunity to access the resources required for its operation. It is the 'structure of the *relations*' that occurs through interaction that gives a social system its form (Parsons 1951: 25; italics in original). If film festival organisers are able to successfully promote a structure of relations that presents the optimum advantages of interaction, it is very likely that resource providers will not only develop an expectation of what the benefits of interaction should be, but will also display a preference for those events that are understood to deliver these benefits. It is this preference that connects the strategy to what is termed Resource Dependency Theory.

Resource Dependency Theory, consistent with Open System Theory, understands organisations to be dependent on their environment for resources (Pfeffer and Salancik 2003) and this is manifested in a festival's reliance upon the resources imported from its participants. Should a film festival achieve the reputation for delivering highly sought-after benefits of interaction, however, it is possible for a resource provider to develop a dependency upon the film festival to perform a particular function. For example, critic Jonathan Rosenbaum indicates the business-based incentives for attending Cannes: 'I wound up meeting more people there in ten days then I'd met in Paris during half a year' (2009: 153). A similar sentiment is expressed by Joe O'Kane of the San Jose Film Commission who maintains that the 'cost for me to come to Cannes is the same as a week or ten days in L.A. and I get more business done' (Beauchamp & Béhar: 310).

When a situation such as this develops, an organisation can be understood to have achieved the height of its organisational power in terms of resource control (Pfeffer and Salancik 2003). In terms of film festival operation, this means that event organisers will then have a greater degree of influence over the importation of resources and may begin to restrict the type of interaction in which the event engages. The Slamdance Film Festival, for example, is able to limit 'submissions to films without domestic theatrical distribution, by first time feature directors, and with relatively low budgets' (Burton 2005). That strategy no doubt helps to rarify the Slamdance experience by offering speciality programming and therefore increasing the incentives for distributors, film critics and first time feature directors to participate.

It is the achievement of this form of reverse dependency and the control it affords film festival organisers that motivates the implementation of this strategy of affiliation. But it is not enough for film festival organisers to simply state the advantages of participation in order for this strategy to take optimal effect. They must instead initiate a process through which the value of interaction becomes obvious to the resource provider in the form of, for example, testimonials for other potential participants. So, when *The New York Times* identifies the Seattle International Film Festival as 'one of the most influential film festivals in the world' (Gore 2001: 324), or *Movie Maker* magazine considers the

U.S.-based Angelus Awards Student Film Festival (www.angelus.org) to be the 'best film festival bet' (Garcelon 2005), this can only serve to validate the importance of these respective film festivals to prospective attendees and participants.

Awards may also be presented and used, like testimonials, to determine the value of participation. Awards can come as monetary payments, as in Japan's Skip City International D-Cinema Festival's (www.skipcity-dcf.jp) awarding of ¥10 million [US $119,650] as a first prize in 2005 (Frater 2005); but awards have also taken the form of original French paintings (Beauchamp and Béhar 1992: 357), or even land in the high desert of Taos, New Mexico (Gore 2001: 330). The most important aspect of such awards is that they must be useful to the recipient; they must provide gratification. For some, awards are only of value if they 'can give a leg up to a new director who could almost certainly use the cash, [then] cash is more valuable than some hideous statuette!' (Rayns 2009: 91). Certainly other incentives exist, and some will be discussed below, but it is generally agreed that 'the best way for festivals to work to attract the films that they want is with, no doubt, cold hard cash' (Peranson 2009: 32).

Incentives may be reputation-based. Awards, or even just acceptance by a particular film festival, provide a kind of branding for marketing purposes (de Valck 2007: 112) and such 'brands' are intrinsically connected to film festivals' role as 'sites of passage', which serve as 'gateways to cultural legitimization' (Idem: 38). Distributors, filmmakers and sales agents will actively search out and enter those festivals that represent, through their identifiable functions or legitimizing affiliations, a cultural seal of approval. Reputations can be made by merely fraternising at particular events. As Ebert describes, 'critics meet again and again during the festival [Cannes], at luncheons and dinners and cocktail receptions and parties' (1987: 90). A good meal and a couple of drinks usually form the basis for an effective participation-based incentive.

Given the differing individual reasons for participating in any event, the variety of incentives available to promote resource provider interaction is potentially boundless. But this also means that some incentive-based strategies may not be applicable given the structure of the particular film festival and those resource providers who may be involved. Filmmakers often inform Mark Fishkin of the Mill Valley Film Festival that they would be more likely to participate in that event if it were competitive and gave awards (Fishkin 2009c: 27). This is a situation that can put tremendous pressure on an organiser to incorporate competitive aspects into their film festival so as to better suit the needs of the participants. Still, Tim Highsted notes that while awards may increase the number of entries into a film festival, facilitating a competition is often challenging:

> It's expensive to run, and it's complicated in terms of how the jury's going to operate, and how fair the system of judging is going to be. You have a lot to deal with, like: What sort of awards are you going to get, where's the money going to come from, is it going to be a cash award, is there a 'uniqueness' to the awards, are you simply going to give the 'best films', or an 'audience award'? You have to think through what the award structure is going to be and why you've got it. (Highsted 2009: 48)

And the addition of a competition may actually be to the detriment of the film festival, because most competitions are aimed at non-established filmmakers and so tend to dissuade known filmmakers from participating. Ron Henderson describes how he had to make personal contact with Woody Allen to assure the filmmaker that the Denver International Film Festival was non-competitive:

> I had to write him, personally assuring him that our festival was not a competitive festival, before he would even let his films open the fest. There's a strong feeling among some artists that they don't want to have anything to do with competitive festivals. (Henderson 2009: 123; emphasis in original)

Film festival organisers may similarly develop a film market or distribution arm in an attempt to gain more business-related film industry attention. For example, the Moscow International Film Festival (moscowfilmfestival. ru/eng) is reported to have appointed an 'industry officer in an effort to stimulate business' (Birchenough 2005). While such activities may draw good attendances – over 8,000 people participate in the Cannes-affiliated Le Marché du Cinéma (de Valck 2007: 113) – there are no guarantees that they will actually generate additional participation for that particular event. Emile Fallaux describes how CineMart, the International Film Festival Rotterdam's film market, 'didn't get attention' for its first twelve years (Fallaux 2009: 57). Simon Field, who replaced Fallaux as director at Rotterdam, notes that the distribution arm of the festival faces similar difficulties because 'energy is used up trying to do distribution, when it could be used to rethink how some sections of the festival should work' (Field 2009: 71).

The effective implementation of a participation-based strategy begins with a need for interaction. The first assessment film festival organisers should conduct is a determination of the demand that exists for the film festival's particular services (Fishkin 2009b: 20). This is done in order to understand the likelihood of resource provider participation. Without recognition of the provision of a viable function, it is highly unlikely that film festival organisers will be able to motivate enough resource importation to sustain operation, regardless of the use of importation-based strategies.

Once a demand for a particular service is identified, film festival organisers may then implement participation-based incentives aimed at those participants who are most critical to operation. Such incentives construct a frame specifically designed to promote the benefits of participation, as with the Washington-based Edmonds International Film Festival (www.edmondsfilmfestival.com) in America, which advertises its ability to arrange 'four scheduled-for-you meetings in Hollywood with a reputable, recognized manager, an agent and two production companies, plus cash' for winners of its awards (Gore 2001: 274). Similarly, Beauchamp and Béhar detail the 'hierarchical order' according to which access passes are conferred on participants at Cannes, explaining how the 'laminated badges of diverse colours' become status symbols by clearly demarcating the levels at which participants are allowed to engage in the film festival activities (1992: 231). The strategy of enforcing this hierarchy enables Cannes to motivate those highly sought-after resource providers to participate, by affording them special privileges, status and prestige, so that the 'white pass is bestowed upon those exalted few who both review films for important publications and cover the social arm of the festival as well' (1992: 232).

Film festivals are undeniably 'manufactured spectacles' (Brown 2009: 220) and the implementation of the strategy of providing participation-based incentives only contributes to such a perception. And as Pfeffer and Salancik explain such 'manufacturing' can have its drawbacks because needing to be cognisant of

> competing demands, even if correctly perceived, makes the management of organizations difficult. It is clearly easier to satisfy a single criterion, or mutually compatible set of criteria, than to attempt to meet the conflicting demands of a variety of participants. (2003: 261)

Most of the time film festival organisers must decide which resource providers to target, with a full understanding that there may be a critical backlash from other potential resource providers. So, disapproval of the

New York Film Festival was expressed by film critics who viewed the promotional status of some of the films, which exempted them from being reviewed, as somewhat restrictive (Hamid 2009: 77); the incentives offered to secure the films from distributors meant that the film festival offered to serve solely as a promotional platform and so pose no risk to the films' theatrical profits. Yet, because the critics were unable to review some of the films, they were, in turn, unable to perform their jobs and, as a consequence, their incentive to participate in the event was greatly diminished.

A festival organiser must never assume that there is a one-size-fits-all solution to such problems; there are as many individual fixes as there are individual participants. Even an audience, which is usually spoken of as a single body of people, is a heterogeneous entity whose individual members must be provided with sympathetically diverse incentives to participate. Gilles Jacob, former director of Cannes, explains that there is 'not one public in Cannes, but several. Australians may love a movie that Scandinavians will hate. We must offer as wide a range as possible, from the most popular to the most difficult' (Beauchamp and Béhar 1992: 54). A similar division can be found among filmmakers. Gore notes that filmmakers often have different criteria to determine the value of participation than other participants (2001: 21) and not all filmmakers perceive the benefits of interaction in the same way. For example, producer Mark Altman explains how 'word of mouth' created by a screening at Cannes helped promote the film *Free Enterprise* (Robert Meyer Burnett, U.S., 1998) (Gore 2001: 141), while Biskind explains that Steven Soderbergh was 'worried that the good word of mouth his film was generating would backfire' (2004: 40).

Knowing what floats the participants' boats will save time and energy. Participation-based incentives are a stark reminder of the contingency of social organisations and relationships reflected in film festivals. Whether it is the handing out of free T-shirts at late night 'exclusive' screenings or the wining and dining of a celebrity filmmaker, it is important that a festival organiser is cognisant of the particular desires and requirements of particular participants and resource providers.

Strategy Seven: Exercise Resource Control

Resource control refers to the influence film festival organisers endeavour to impose over the stimulation and production of resources from the environment and their eventual importation into an event. In places where film financing is limited, this strategy is exercised through the engagement of numerous festival-supported film funds, e.g. the World Cinema Fund or the Hubert Bals Fund, that facilitate filmmaking and which film festivals utilise to further their roles as exhibitors. That is, upon their completion films are often subsequently programmed into their sponsoring festival, thereby developing an alternative importation stream which has been dubbed, not too tastefully, 'fest incest' by many festival professionals. Critic Ron Holloway explains that 'fest incest is a festival funding formula that works like a charm', and notes its common practice among major European film festivals (Wall 2009).

Pfeffer and Salancik present a definition of control as 'the ability to initiate or terminate actions at one's discretion' (2003: 259) that – while it is useful in its breadth of applicability – can be misleading in its implications of authority. The control which this strategy attempts to manufacture can never be absolute because the importation of resources from the environment cannot be guaranteed; the complexities associated with participating in a social system and the film festival's very position as a site of exhibition greatly reduces assurances that a resource will definitely be available, so reliance upon this single input, regardless of any apparent and ostensible level of control is a dangerous move.

Resource control may be used by film festivals to influence the importation of resources in three ways. First, through the manufacturing of resources by the festival itself, as with events such as the multi-national 48-Hour Film Project (www.48hourfilm.com), which requires filmmaking participants to accomplish 'all creativity' (2012), including script creation, production and post-production, within a designated 48-hour time period, in order for their work to be eligible for submission. The Australian Tropfest (www.tropfest.com) requires that a particular 'signature item' such as dice or an umbrella (or even just a reference to that item) be included in each submitted film (Tropfest 2008). According to the Tropfest organisers, the item is intended to 'stimulate and inspire people and to encourage filmmakers to hone their craft, not just drag out last year's work' (Ibid.). Each of these film festivals arguably influences the creation of new, unique resources specific to their individual event, thereby successfully initiating the production of resources required for their own operations.

This technique is observable on a much larger scale with regard to the film funds just mentioned. The World Cinema Fund (WCF), for example, is a partnership between the German Federal Cultural Foundation, the Goethe-Institut and the Berlin International Film Festival, that aims to 'help the realisation of films which otherwise could not be produced' (Berlin Film Festival 2009b). Through the WCF, filmmakers from select geographical areas are awarded up to €100,000 (US$133,000) to assist with their film projects. The stipulation that each project must have a German production company partner attached, establishes parameters of production analogous to those of Tropfest and the 48-Hour Film Project – and simultaneously serves to provide participation-based incentives to the favoured German production companies. Although direct entry into the film festival is an officially-stated requirement, the connection between the WCF and the Berlin International Film Festival is evident: the WCF homepage is part of the Berlin Festival's website, thoroughly branding the fund as part of the film festival; and films produced through the WFC are listed as part of the film festival's programme, indicating the first option the festival has for screening any suitable films. In fact, four films from the WFC were awarded the top prizes at Berlin in 2009, suggesting a definite connection between the films produced by the cinema fund, its affiliated film festival, and participants.

The second method by which resource control may influence the importation of resources is through the restriction of secured resources, which sees film festival organisers accepting resources only under conditions of exclusivity. Simon Field explains that many competitions require that they be able to present a film's première screening and are thus able to effectively limit the number of resources in the environment available to their competitors, effectively starving the competition of the resource race and contributing to the operations-driven entropy of other, competing film festivals. According to Field:

> When we talk about Toronto, Rotterdam, Cannes, they're all competing with each other and we know now that Toronto is very much preoccupied with world premieres. Rumour has it that it prevents other festivals from getting films, which is characteristic of every festival that wants to have premieres, to stop others from getting them first. (Field 2009: 59)

Some film festivals have been less covert in their desire for exclusivity. The organisers of the Melbourne International Film Festival for example placed a clause in the festival's entry form preventing programmed films from being screened elsewhere in the country prior to the festival (MIFF 2012). Similarly, the entry form and regulations for the 18th Australian Flickerfest (www.flickerfest.com.au) states that, due to the festival's 'competitive nature', any 'Australian films selected for competition must not have been screened in Sydney within 6 months of the festival dates' (Flickerfest 2009).

Such restrictions provide organisers with evidence of the importance and consequent value of their event that may be presented to other resource providers – sponsors, critics, audience members – in order to stimulate their motivation to participate in such a unique event; this is to succumb to what has been termed 'premiere-itis' (Koehler

2009: 86). According to Koehler, 'festivals yearn to draw as much press as possible and premiering films constitute news' (2009: 86). It is typical, he says, for film festival boards 'to measure success partly on the metric of the number of premières pulled off, and therefore pressure the director and programmers to come up with a sufficient quota of them for each edition' (Ibid.). Emile Fallaux confirms this tendency by noting that most programmers attend only those film festivals 'where [they] can expect new material' (Fallaux 2009: 51).

Programming plays the central role in film festival functionality and is often the first resource that is scrutinised by potential participants when determining an event's importance. News that the films in competition at the Locarno International Film Festival were the 'weakest in several years' was used to open media reports of that event (Elley 2004), supporting the claim that 'ultimately [a festival] must stand or fall on the quality of its programming' (Webber 2005). The perception that a film festival is not attracting the best films can have devastating effects and promote both financial and participation-driven entropy. Film festival organisers can counter this possibility by taking pre-emptive action should there be any doubt regarding the quality of programming. Marco Müller, for example, held a press conference soon after his appointment as director of the Venice International Film Festival to announce the event had 'been offered quite a few films from the U.S. as world premieres', thus dispelling the notion the festival would lack its traditionally perceived value due to a shortened programming period (Vivarelli 2004).

The need to obtain unique films is also illustrated by those festivals that resort to the screening of unfinished films. For example, programming at the 2004 Tribeca Film Festival included 'a 20-minute exclusive preview' of the animated feature *Shark Tale* (Bibo Bergeron, Vicky Jenson, Rob Letterman, U.S., 2004) (Amdur and Rooney 2004) which would not be released in its completed form until later that year. Similarly, Harris notes that the screening of 'works in progress' (2004a) such as *The Libertine* (Laurence Dunmore, U.S., 2004) at the Toronto International Film Festival, is becoming more acceptable and thus provides a newly-available programming stream for some film festivals.

The third way in which resource control influences importation involves, once again, a festival's character as a social system. The concept of participant obligation stems from the personal connection an individual participant may have to a film festival. It has been observed that film festival organisers will often create 'an ongoing supply relationship with *auteurs* whose films they showcase on an exclusive basis' (Iordanova 2009: 26). This enables film festival organisers to not only successfully overcome programming shortages; it also gives festivals exclusive access to much-desired resources. An example of the former is the fact that the majority of the Australian films programmed for the early Sydney Film Festival were supplied by individuals serving on the event's organising committee (Hope 2004: 61). In the case of the latter, Beauchamp and Béhar comment that the Cannes Film Festival 'played a pivotal role in the career of Ingrid Bergman' (1992: 27), causing her to display a personal preference towards the festival. This allowed the event exclusive access to the star and such favouring was made manifest in the actress' participation as the president of the festival's jury in 1973.

Film festival organisers must 'nurture relationships' (Bowser 2009: 140). A nurturing relationship can be established through the film funds that provide filmmakers with their 'big break', as when the Thessaloniki International Film Festival-sponsored Balkan Fund offered facilitation for award recipients to begin 'their international career' (Kerkinos 2009: 171), or through festival workshops that present opportunities for aspiring filmmakers to participate in programs such as the Berlinale Talent Campus. It is through 'on-the-spot training, [that] festivals help new talents prepare for the transnational practice of the contemporary film industry' (de Valck 2007: 109). Provision of such training not only develops a personal connection between the participant and the festival, but also increases the likelihood that the participant will be successful in their chosen career path, and thereby be able to later provide a reciprocal flow of resources via legitimizing affiliation in the form of patronage as noted above. This has the potential to, in turn, motivate a fresh supply of critics, filmmakers, producers, etc., who will also be open to future interaction; a real investment in the future.

It is important to note once again, however, that the contrived nature of social systems serves to ensure that a participant's commitment to a film festival will not necessarily be permanent. Cousins discusses the tenuous nature of relationships and simultaneously illustrates the unpredictability of dealing with individuals in social systems:

> Cannes tends its relationship with Pedro Almodovar with great care but if he doesn't win the Palm d'Or there soon, might he switch allegiances to Venice? Venice has, for years, been the festival of choice for Woody Allen but might Toronto or Berlin be making approaches behind the scenes? (2009: 155)

The same may be said of sponsors: everyone is a friend until they decide differently. In 2009, the main sponsor of the Berlin International Film Festival, Volkswagen, terminated its seven-year long sponsorship of the festival due to financial difficulties. The withdrawal reflected a '30 per cent drop in film festivals' sponsorship revenue' (Roddick 2009: 167) that occurred as a result of the global financial crisis and clearly demonstrates the fickle nature of resource control. It is for this reason that the Vancouver International Film Festival works towards securing 'multi-year sponsorship' (SECOR 2004: 49) in order to enable the organisers to gain a degree of control over the withdrawal of resources.

Strategy Eight: Join the Club

By adopting specific codes of practice into their operational structure, film festivals can become eligible for accreditation by, or membership of an external organisation. This in turn identifies the film festival as being a preferred site of exhibition to various resource providers, including film producers, distributors, film critics, guild members and the members of different academies, and it serves to encourage their participation by enhancing their perception of the probability of gratification.

In a manner similar to the employment of legitimizing affiliations, approval by a sanctioning organisation validates the functional purpose of the film festival. This is a concept acknowledged by organisational behaviour theorists DiMaggio and Powell, who note how 'professional and trade associations provide other arenas in which center organizations [in this case, film festivals] are recognized' (1988: 86). This recognition is, however, fundamentally different to that gained through legitimizing affiliations, in that it is entirely driven by external factors.

Film festivals currently function under two types of sanctioning organisations. The first type governs film festival activity and includes organisations such as the Fédération Internationale des Associations de Producteurs de Films (International Federation of Film Producers Associations (FIAPF)), the Belgium-based European Fantastic Film Festivals Federation (EFFFF), the European Co-ordination of Film Festival (ECFF) and the U.K.-based Universal Film and Festival Organization (UFFO). These organisations set their own standards for film festival operation, which organisers must implement in order to be eligible for accreditation. Adopting these external standards into a film festival links the event to the additional resource importation-based opportunities that accreditation presents through designated supply channels (e.g. members of the organisation), and by the prestige and appearance of exclusivity affiliation provides. Indeed, accreditation by FIAPF has been explicitly noted as being 'not simply a means of obtaining high-quality European releases, [but] also a way of maintaining the higher status and prestige' necessary to set a festival apart from others seeking resources from the same operating environment (Hope 2004: 228).

Sanctioning by this particular type of organisation represents recognised operational accountability and, as such, is likely to improve resource importation because it presents to participants the expectation of a known and approved quality of interaction; it says: 'these people are professionals'. The rules imposed by a governing body 'constitute a trust contract between those festivals and the film industry at large' (FIAPF 2010) and present a framework upon which such an assessment may occur. They also build the expectation that such accredited festivals will 'implement quality and reliability standards that meet industry expectations' (Ibid.).

The notion of a 'trust contract' is discussed by organisational theorists John Meyer and Brian Rowan (though not in those terms) who, in their investigation of formal organisational structures, observe that 'many organizations actively seek charters from collective authorities and manage to institutionalize their goals and structures in the rules of such authorities' (1983: 29). Thus, through the implementation of FIAPF's trust contract or the ECFF's 'Code of Ethics', film festival organisers are, in effect, communicating to potential participants a shared set of values and expectations. Without this understanding film festival organisers may encounter resistance from resource providers who do not fully understand their festival's operational practices. Australia's Sydney Film Festival required FIAPF accreditation because 'major film producing nations would not send their films halfway around the world without some protection of their interests' (Webber 2005). Also noteworthy in this sense is a Flanders International Film Festival advertisement announcing the festival as having 'built a strong reputation as the world's very first FIAPF-recognized competitive film event that celebrates music and its impact on film' (Cowie 2002: 345). Overt references to FIAPF accreditation are undoubtedly intended to frame a festival as a unique, important and sanctioned event.

The second type of sanctioning organisation does not govern film festival operation, but rather forms accreditation-based partnerships with film festivals in order to represent their particular special focus/interest. The Fédération Internationale de la Presse Cinématographique (International Federation of Film Critics (FIPRESCI)) is one such organisation whose membership includes 'professional film critics and film journalists, established in different countries for the promotion and development of film culture and for the safeguarding of professional interests' (FIPRESCI 2009). Additional examples of this second type of sanctioning organisation include the Network for the Promotion of Asian Cinema (NETPAC), the Coordinating Anthropological Film Festivals of Europe Organisation (CAFFE) and the International Federation of Film Societies (FICC).

Accreditation by these organisations may be used by film festival organisers to establish their event's legitimacy in terms of film culture and industry rather than through its operational efficiency and structure. When the Chicago International Film Festival is described as 'one of two US sites to award the FIPRESCI prize' (Cowie 2002: 339), such an appellation serves to provide critical value to the festival. That the Stockholm International Film Festival (www.stockholmfilmfestival.se) is lauded as the 'only Scandinavian festival recognized by FIAPF, it hosts a FIPRESCI jury and is also a member of the European Coordination of Film Festivals' (Cowie 2002: 367), indicates the festival as a showcase of quality films and film culture rather than a mere cash cow for participants, and in a manner similar to that accomplished by ascribing an identifiable function. The presence of an international jury made up of FIPRESCI members to award a prize in the name of the organisation can additionally motivate particular resource providers into an interaction with the event.

One of the benefits of this latter type of sanctioning organisation is the direct line of contact that can be established between film festival organisers and those resource providers upon whom the event is most dependent for operation. The International Federation of Film Societies (FICC) publishes 'festival reports' in which members of the organisation discuss programming aspects of a particular film festival; as when one self-proclaimed 'member of the international jury of the FICC' remarks of the Cracow Film Festival (www.krakowfilmfestival.pl/en), that 'I could appreciate [the] richness and diversity of the pictures gathered together during the five day festival' (Lazaruk 2004). The Polish-based International Young Audience Film Festival Ale Kino (www.alekino.com/en), the German International Children's Film Festival LUCAS (www.lucas-filmfestival.de/en) and Finland's Videotivoli Video Festival for Children and Young People (www.videotivoli.fi/english09), are all accredited by the International Centre of Films for Children and Young People (Centre International du Film pour l'Enfance et la Jeunesse (CIFEJ)) (cijef.blogg.org) (Film Festival World 2010). This accreditation provides the festival organiser with access to, and promotion within the CIJEF's membership circle, which includes producers, filmmakers, distributors, broadcasters and other industry specialists who are directly involved in children's programming and production.

It must be noted that non-accreditation does not necessarily mean that a film festival is less effective in its operation. As SECOR Consulting explains, 'FIAPF endorsement is not the only warranty of quality or prestige, and no American event belongs to the [non-specialised competitive category of the] Federation, not even prestigious Sundance' (2004: 17). Steven Gaydos and Derek Elley report that when the Montréal

World Film Festival lost its FIAPF accreditation in 2003 due to its unsanctioned date shift, the film festival officially – if somewhat testily – announced that festival organisers 'did not wish to be "accredited" by an association that has no real authority – over producers, sales agents, distributors or over festivals' (2003). Such an announcement, of course, serves the purpose of declaring the festival master of its own ship in light of a particularly stormy passage, but it also manages to convey the sense that sanctioning organisations are not as crucial to operation as they would like the world to believe.

The 'closed door' policy according to which many sanctioning organisations conduct their business and make their decisions, has led to intense scrutiny of their actual motivations. The FIAPF 'A-list' system of accreditation and festivals have been described as 'pointless' (Cousins 2009: 155), and as examples of 'dull, fading, provincial caricatures of the old red-carpet routines' (Quintín 2009: 42). In the case of the FIAPF endorsement of the Cairo International Film Festival (www.cairofilmfest. org) as one of its 12 A-listed film festivals, it was described as 'the scandal of the Festival circuit' (Roddick 2009: 165). Such animosity towards bodies like FIAPF emanates from the private club feel of the organisation; the seeming self-importance that accompanies inclusion leaves many of those individuals not feted with inclusion feeling scornful and sceptical of the true importance of sanction and validation.

There can be no doubt, though, that there are advantages to be gained by courting sanctioning organisations. Being part of 'the club' can offer a film festival a significant return in terms of securing resources both through membership and through the legitimisation that the affiliation provides. There are benefits, too, in terms of instilling that sense of cultural worth and critical exploration that organisations such as FIPRESCI offer and which enable a film festival to gain prestige that can only come from the approval of an apparent authority.

* * * * * *

Successful film festival management is not rocket science... If it were it might be easier. The unpredictable nature of the film festival environment and the contrived social character of these events ensure that, year in and year out, organisers will face a new set of challenges, all of which will threaten their festival's wellbeing. The purpose of this chapter was to give perspective. Sometimes it is difficult, as the saying goes, to see the forest for the trees. The prolonged nature of film festival operation often blinds organisers to what is really important: the gratification of participants. But gratification is not simply making people happy. It is a process that is dependent upon both the duration and substance of an individual's film festival experience. A filmmaker who only attends an award ceremony will have a different appreciation (or contempt) for an event in comparison with a critic who is present at every screening. Both experiences are legitimate, but the amounts of time and effort spent to achieve such payoffs are worlds apart.

The success of a film festival cannot and should not be wholly quantified. Empirical data recounting profit margins and audience numbers do demonstrate where particular strengths of an event may lie, but ultimately they only serve as benchmarks for participation. The achievement of a complete Open System Paradigm cycle is by far a better measure of efficient operation because it confirms that gratification has been achieved. An ecstatic distributor, who has benefited from the programming, screening and subsequent media coverage that resulted from a festival, is more likely to participate at a deeper level the following year than a lukewarm distributor whose coveted film premièred to an empty theatre and failed to make any headlines due to a lacklustre performance by the event's media department.

The eight strategies identified in this chapter are methods by which film festival organisers are able to assess and increase the likelihood of participation. These strategies range from the physical location of an event to the legitimizing effect organisers, board members, patrons, and other industry personalities may have on film festival operation through their professional or even associational affiliation. High levels of external involvement are indicative of a healthy Open System. Simply put, the more choices there are, the better the chances of achieving operational stability and being able to do the whole thing again the following year.

These strategies are not fool-proof and require careful consideration by organisers to ensure their effectiveness. It is quite possible for one film festival to utilise only a handful of strategies while another event employs all eight; this is the individual nature of film festival operation. To prove this point the next chapter is dedicated to a case study of an occasion in which all strategies were used to revive a defunct film festival and re-establish gratification among its disillusioned participants.

Chapter 4
Case Study:
The Gold Coast Film Fantastic

Ever seen a dead film festival? It's not a pretty sight. The office lies in tatters with half-written reports and first-draft thank you letters hastily cut and pasted from pre-existing documents and minimised on computer desktops; rolled up posters stand in corners and packets of promotional T-shirts lie mouldering on the paper-strewn carpet. An eerie funereal atmosphere pervades the space. Here is a life cut tragically short, its full potential never reached; had things only been different it would still be here with us today.

This is the story of a clinically dead film festival that rose from its ashes to once again shine its light on cinema screens. It is a triumphant example of the way in which a logical organisational structure (and some creative managerial solutions) became the means through which to develop a sustainable film festival framework. It is a narrative in two parts. Let the tale begin.

Australia's Gold Coast is an ideal place to host a film festival. Beautiful white sandy beaches, an assortment of nightlife activities, a major motion picture production studio only minutes away. In fact, few places in the world can match the possibilities presented by the Gold Coast. Located in southern Queensland, along nearly 40 miles of clear water beaches, this sprawling city covers a whopping 541 square miles. The majority of its 50,000-plus inhabitants can be found living in a string of beachside suburbs that run parallel to the Coral Sea. For the most part, 'Coasties' – an odd blend of conservative retirees and young party animals – inhabit a world that is predictable, relaxing and pretty well flushed with cash.

Film scholars, culturally-minded city council members and local film luminaries first toyed with the idea of a Gold Coast film festival in 1996 and, after forming a steering committee, these early event architects began to cobble together their ideal festival modelled on major international film festivals in Europe, Asia and the United States.

Such lofty goals for an event are not uncommon among film festival organisers; everyone wants their own Cannes. Yet, for the most part, the cultural aspects of life on the Gold Coast enjoy a modest patronage. Interested individuals are able to take advantage of live shows and music at the Gold Coast Arts Centre, Jupiter's Casino or other various smaller private venues. But this is a land of sun, sand and surf, and so going to the movies is something done primarily when the tide is out or on those few days that it rains; in which case there are several commercial theatres and a well-programmed art house cinema that caters to those with non-mainstream cinematic tastes. Beyond this handful of outlets there almost seems to be a phobia of the Arts. Perhaps this is why even the phrase *film festival* was left out of the event's official title.

Add to this the region's hosting of major annual sporting events such as the ANZ Ladies Master Golf, the Pan-Pacific Masters Games, the Gold Coast Airport Marathon, the Indy 300 and the Conrad Jupiter's Magic Millions Carnival and it can easily be understood that in order for an event to survive on the Gold Coast it must be big and relatively palatable to mass consumer tastes. Other prerequisites include that an event should be blessed with star patrons, be capable of major media coverage and, most importantly, put a lot of heads in Gold Coast beds (tourism is such a mainstay that in recent years nearly 10 million visitors – half the national population – have travelled to the region annually for vacation purposes). In effect then, it is the event that creates the biggest splash that wins the majority of the attention and council funding. So it was not surprising that the steering committee opted to dangle visions of star-studded red carpets and exclusive world film premières before the eyes the city's decision makers.

Not surprisingly, unrealistic expectations caused more harm than good. The festival's presumed role in enhancing the local creative sector and contributing massively to the local film industry and economy created a blown out image of the event that was impossible to sustain. For such an ambitious undertaking, it was of primary importance to involve two of Australia's most prominent film industry organisations, the Screen Producers Association of Australia (www.spaa.org.au) (SPAA) and the Australian Film Institute (AFI) (www.afi.org.au). It was a paradoxical situation, since for either partnership to happen it was essential to secure substantial sponsorship support and in order to secure such substantial sponsorship there would need to be some guarantee that the festival would have a key position in the Australian context, which was impossible unless there was a sizeable sponsor on board, and so on… Since Australia already played host to three major international film festivals: in Melbourne (since 1951), Sydney (since 1954) and just up the road in Brisbane (since 1992), this was going to be a difficult task. These were (and still are) well-established festivals, and proving that the Gold Coast event was a better option for the film industry or other sponsors would be difficult at best.

Coincidentally, during the two years (1996-7) that the steering committee was wallowing in the mire of pre-festival proposals and production, a new international film festival appeared on the Sunshine Coast, 150km (90 miles) to the north. The Noosa Film Festival (NFF) represented the type of world class film industry event that the steering committee on the Gold Coast was hoping to facilitate and was accompanied by some impressive opening gambits – the official launch of the film festival was held in Los Angeles and the NFF organisers announced publicly that they had successfully negotiated with international marketing executives, sourced films from large festivals and formed alliances with the leaders in the festival world.

For all intents and purposes, the NFF seemed to have beaten the Gold Coast event to the punch and looked likely to be crowned Australia's hot new festival. Not only would the Sunshine Coast event have Hollywood stars and a total income of AUD$2.5 million (US$2.4 million), but it also boasted a much-coveted array of prominent sponsors that included Polo Ralph Lauren, Showtime, *Who Weekly Magazine*, SAAB and Kodak Australia (Globe Entertainment 2000: 5).

But things were not as they seemed and while the Gold Coast festival was still reeling at this new entry into their environment (and just to prove how certain it is that uncertainty will prevail in human affairs), the NFF suffered a massive economic coronary and died almost instantly. It seems that the NFF organisers had not fully secured the inputs from their financial participants before outputting them, and a string of sudden sponsorship withdrawals left the event sputtering entropically with significant debt. The Noosa Film Festival failed to complete its first edition and was never heard of again.

The ramifications of the NFF collapse were immediate and long lasting. The film festival scorched the film industry environment like a raging wildfire. All planning for the Gold Coast film festival would now have to exercise – and be seen to be exercising – extreme care and caution in its courting of those same key participants who had been burned by the failed event.

Gone were the notions of a new high profile industry event. Instead the film festival would be non-competitive and feature programming that 'explored the many facets of "fantasy", including horror, sci-fi, special effects, thriller movies, animation, fantasy, film noir, magical realism and so on' (Globe Entertainment 2000: 13). The event now planned was to follow in the footsteps of several established 'fantasy' festivals, including the Brussels International Fantastic Film Festival (BIFFF) (www. festivalfantastique.org/festival) in Belgium, the South Korean Puchon International Fantastic Film Festival (www.pifan.com), the Fantasporto:

Oporto International Film Festival (www.fantasporto.online.pt/uk) in Portugal and the Donostia-San Sebastian Horror and Fantasy Film Festival in Spain (http://www.donostiakultura.com/terror/2012) (Ibid.). To accompany this new direction, the event was given a formal title: the Gold Coast Film Fantastic (GCFF).

There was a rationale behind this new focus: no other Australian film festivals featured fantasy films exclusively and so the GCFF would not need to compete for programming. It would also be differentiated from other Australian film festivals, thereby increasing incentives in some quarters to participate in the event. Additionally, the focus on fantasy would apparently afford the GCFF organisers 'the opportunity to concentrate on the "people behind the scenes"' (Globe Entertainment 2000: 15). That is, it would enable GCFF to secure the participation of highly-qualified film industry practitioners who were not necessarily in high demand and were therefore more likely to interact. This actually proved to be the case and two prominent Gold Coast-based film industry practitioners John Cox (1995, Visual Effects Academy Award® winner for *Babe* (Chris Noonan, Australia, U.S., 1995)) and Peter Frampton (1995, Make-up Academy Award® winner for *Braveheart* (Mel Gibson, U.S., 1995)) were positioned as the event's patrons. The affiliation with these two Oscar® winners not only gave the event prestige and legitimacy within the film industry, but also contributed to securing the identity of the event as a fantasy film festival. These would prove to be vital connections in the formation of proposed festival addenda such as make-up workshops and panel discussions.

In 2002 the Gold Coast Film Fantastic was instituted; and for the most part it seemed that the event would find some success after having secured modest seed funding from the Gold Coast City Council. However, the transition from planning on paper to projecting film prints is never easy and the ideas and concepts that flowed in the early planning stages suddenly became snagged on technical operational hitches. It is moments like these that require a 'talented artistic director who usually makes the big difference for the festival having some ultimate degree of success, or even survival' (Gilmore 2009: 136). Unfortunately, no such figure was forthcoming and though it may be difficult for some readers to comprehend, the Gold Coast Film Fantastic actually operated for four consecutive editions (2002-5) without a designated film festival director. Rather, the GCFF board appointed individuals with PR backgrounds to facilitate the event.

This reportedly led to misunderstandings over the actual requirements of the position and the amount of work the job entailed. As a result, the festival was run by a string of project managers who did not want to renew their contracts, and a board that became increasingly disenchanted with the very idea of facilitating a film festival at all. The principal flaw that led to this outcome was the idiosyncratic nature of the festival as a one-person-show. That is, the board believed the individual hired as the project manager should be able to fulfil all festival tasks ranging from media coverage to film programming to volunteer coordination to guest relations management etc. with little or no external help.

The turnover of managers meant that with each new appointment the GCFF would lose the social connectivity that had been built among the participants in the current and previous cycles, systematically isolating potentially valuable input sources by shifting its allegiance from one management group to the next. So each film festival edition represented a re-building rather than a continuation of operation, and key open system aspects such as feedback were not heeded or actioned because valuable information regarding previous participant perceptions of the festival was lost with every departure.

In 2006, the GCFF successfully hired its first experienced festival director. This person had a proven track record and had facilitated a local, community-based short film festival as well as a national travelling film festival. The benefits of hiring this individual were immediately apparent: meetings were arranged with three major Australian distributors, ensuring an interpersonal relationship between the film festival and its content suppliers. Where in the past, distributors would generally be approached via e-mail or phone, the fact that the new festival director flew interstate specifically to meet each of them personally not only indicated the value the festival placed on distributors' participation, but also enabled the director to address any particular concerns regarding operation immediately. The festival director was also active in the recruitment of several new board members, including a local commercial cinema venue manager. My own involvement occurred after I was approached by this director and had listened to his inspiring ideas for the event; I agreed to put forth my candidacy to join the board. I was immediately voted onto the board due to the growing expertise of film festival operation I was gaining at a local university. To my surprise, due to the low state of morale among veteran board members, I was elected the festival chair.

In the beginning everything went well. With the appointment of the new festival director the event appeared to have someone suited to the role, someone who understood the complications associated with film festival management. Yet unfortunately, the newly hired director stepped down from the festival's helm, for personal reasons, immediately after the completion of the 2006 edition.

This was a serious dent in leadership and had several detrimental effects. First and most importantly, there was minimal re-energisation of the film festival environment: acquittal forms detailing the festival's performance were submitted late to the relevant funding organisations (or not at all); follow-up acknowledgement to patrons and special guests and expressions of thanks for their participation were a long time coming, and when they did eventuate were decidedly – even insultingly – generic; the 2006 Festival Report was a lacklustre document that did not contain any empirical data such as audience attendance figures or economic impact statements of the event by which participants could assess the level of gratification they had received from the event. In short, the resignation resulted in the loss of all the open system advantages the director had facilitated, and this placed the GCFF in a decidedly worse position than before.

I must take some responsibility for this particular setback of the Gold Coast Film Fantastic. During my one-year appointment as the festival's chair I watched as the environment continually grew colder to the idea of a film festival. Excitement levels dropped both within and outside of the organisation and it seemed that positive achievements were immediately swallowed by an overwhelming sense of the inevitability that one would be unable to deliver the grandiose event predicted by the steering committee. So, on a rare overcast day in winter, a quorum of board members met and decided to euthanase the festival. No programming would be entered into, no funding would be sought and no films would be screened. We would effectively place the film festival on life support by freezing all spending and operational activity other than that needed for the GCFF web domain and for the annual dues required by the Australian Securities and Investments Commission. By all measures the film festival was clinically dead and no date was set for another board meeting.

But of course that is not how the story ends. In the great stories and myths of the ages, the hero experiences death and, through the wisdom and self-knowledge that comes from this experience, is able to continue and ultimately complete the quest. It is probably not giving too much away to declare that this particular hero – the Gold Coast Film Fantastic – did indeed rise from its own ashes and ultimately go on to fulfil its destiny as a festival of film.

After several months of careful consideration, I volunteered for the position of Gold Coast Film Fantastic festival director and, drawing up a 72-page project proposal, I presented my arguments to the board, indicating what I considered to be the correct course for the film festival. This included such aspirations as expanding the programming focus and encouraging more community-based activities. There was little resistance to my ideas and a vote was passed that I should use the remaining AUD$25,000 (US$24,066) to jumpstart the event. Still, as I left the meeting I sensed that not all was right, that instead of sparking a general feeling of satisfaction that we, as a board, had managed to stand by the event, I was overcome with sudden anxiety about the loneliness of my position.

This was to be my festival. I had volunteered to lead it. All decisions, all the work and all blame would fall on me. The board members would support me only as long as their own reputations were not diminished in any way, shape or form. Over the course of the next few weeks I met with various individuals, institutions and cultural agencies in order to gauge their receptiveness towards the film festival, and assess the state of the environment. I then began to implement an operational plan that I believed would reactivate the event.

My first course of action was to create two new programming streams in the belief that the original idea of screening only fantasy films was a two-edged sword. Certainly the festival would be one of the first ports of call for filmmakers as it provided an exclusive outlet for the genre in Australia. Yet, the number of fantasy films produced is limited and fluctuates, so programming a full slate of quality films could prove difficult. Most importantly, fantasy films did not appeal to the retirees, a large proportion of the demographic of the Gold Coast community. In fact, the steering committee's initial decision to focus only on fantasy was based on the assumption that fans of the genre were 'fanatical followers, who, evidently will travel to such events' (Globe Entertainment 2000: 15).

This view of the festival's audience was fundamentally flawed. Of course 'traveling fanatics' will, if they arrive, tick the heads-on-Gold-Coast-beds box, but to rely on an 'if you build it, they will come' attitude is not the proper way to manage any project and was indicative of an aggressive tourism agenda that had little or no regard for the event's other participants. The two new programming streams entailed the inclusion of sports film and locally produced features. The incorporation of sports films was a means of diversifying and expanding both audience and sponsorship participation because sports are a particularly strong pre-occupation of the Australian and Gold Coast psyche and lifestyle. By incorporating sports films into the event there came the opportunity to broaden the GCFF's potential audience base.

The sporting theme also presented the possibility of a new viable income stream from sponsorship. Alternative sponsors needed to be enlisted because previous GCFF editions and the festival's unpredictability had exhausted the supply of fantasy/film industry-based businesses available for participation, leaving few, if any, new areas for funding-based development. According to a 2006 Gold Coast Business Survey, 'just under ninety per cent (88.9%) of [the over 500-square mile region's sports-related] businesses had their head office in the Gold Coast City area' (Gold Coast City Council 2006). This was important information. Not only did it indicate an established sports industry presence; it also proved the ease of contact locally. This then provided an advantage in terms of presenting sponsorship as supportive of a community organisation.

The addition of local feature films was intended to take advantage of a growing number of Gold Coast-based filmmakers. I was aware of several local feature films and believed incorporation of these works would give the GCFF a vibrant new connection to the real Gold Coast film industry. It also had the potential to strengthen the connection between the film festival and the area's film schools.

The time of this reactivation coincided with my own realisation of and growing dedication to the applicability of Open System Theory to film festival management – as an Open System Paradigm. I came to understand that the film festival required new participants because the old resource channels were reluctant to become heavily involved in an on-again-off-again festival. I began to systematically approach various participants whose involvement I felt would nicely complement the event. This was achieved by applying the eight importation-based strategies towards a festival's re-energisation outlined in the previous chapter. The following sections detail how each of these strategies was implemented and notes their respective outcomes with regard to getting the Gold Coast Film Fantastic back on its feet.

Building Alliances

The strategy of building co-operative alliances proved to be instrumental in positioning the GCFF to gain access to a larger, more diverse group of participants. As we have seen, new resource importation streams were required to replace previous participants no longer willing to collaborate in light of their less-than-encouraging involvement with the festival in its previous manifestations. To this end, a total of six co-operative alliances were formed with various community groups, local government initiatives and non-profit organisations.

Chart 1 identifies each of these six alliances, outlining the strategic benefits of each partnership and the resultant shared activities and events that took place during the 10-month lead-up period to the actual operation of the festival. The order in which these strategies are presented is not intended to suggest any hierarchy or preference, since each alliance was equally important in establishing and strengthening the social connectivity of the GCFF overall.

Event timing

The Gold Coast Film Fantastic 2008 was scheduled to run for five days, from 16 October to 20 October. These particular dates were chosen for three strategic reasons. First, the holding of the event in October provided a 10-month period in which to establish new and to re-activate previous inputs for the funding of the festival. For example, the fostering of co-operative alliances began in January to enable eligibility for funding opportunities that spanned from February to July. Processing times and administrative delays would preclude any applications to funding programmes after July, so after that date the only potential income would originate from private sponsorships.

Additionally, this 10-month timeframe permitted the film festival to facilitate projects designed to raise awareness and re-establish the event's reputation. The integration in late June of a 'Fantastic Sneak Peeks' festival preview into the Gold Coast Bazaar – an annual event organised by the local tourism board – centred on the Australian première of *The Ruins* (Carter Smith, U.S., 2008) provided ideal timing for the beginning of a more aggressive campaign to raise the profile of the GCFF. Within two weeks another 'Fantastic Sneak Peeks' was organised, this time featuring Queensland's première of the 1968 Olympics documentary *Salute* (Matt Norman, Australia, U.S., 2008) for the sports-mad population. So, five months prior to the film festival proper, the GCFF had begun to receive broad press coverage and was demonstrating a new and improved functional capacity as an event through the successful integration of a sports-themed film and two premières.

October also positioned the GCFF at an opportune time in relation to the Australian film distribution patterns by providing access to titles set for release during December's summer holidays, thus broadening the festival's programming range. Additionally, with the Australian International Movie Convention being scheduled just a month before the GCFF, I was able to preview and negotiate last-minute programme selections, such as an appropriate opening night film, the Australian première of *Ghost Town* (David Keopp, U.S., 2008).

The third reason for this October timing was to ensure that the opening of the festival did not conflict with any other popular community events. The GCFF was to start two weeks after the school holidays and one week prior to both the Indy 300 car race and the Rugby League World Cup. This placement meant that the film festival would

Chart 1: The 2008 GCFF co-operative alliances

Organisation Name	Description	Co-operative Alliance	Importation-based Benefits
Active and Healthy Gold Coast	A local government, exercise-based programme aimed at promoting active lifestyles among members of the Gold Coast community.	This co-operative alliance connected the functional roles of GCFF as an exhibitor of sports films and as a facilitator of youth-based activities involving new media and sports.	Benefits of alignment ranged from publicity (both printed and virtual) of GCFF community activities, to demonstrating the versatility and importance GCFF could play within the social network of the Gold Coast community thus allowing the event to be viewed as more than just a film festival.
Broadbeach Alliance	A not-for-profit organisation that facilitates entertainment within the Gold Coast suburb of Broadbeach, with the express purpose of attracting people to the suburb for the benefit of local businesses.	This co-operative alliance consisted of a free public screening of the surfing film Endless Summer (Bruce Brown, U.S., 1966).	Endless Summer (Bruce Brown, U.S., 1966) was screened two weeks prior to the actual festival and was able to raise the awareness level of the upcoming film festival via onscreen advertising, media coverage and flyer hand-outs. This co-operative alliance also enabled GCFF to gain access to a new audience demographic: due to the outdoor and admission-free nature of the screening, audience members in the form of families with young children, who otherwise may not participate in a festival, were provided with an opportunity to interact with and contribute to the overall community impact of the film festival.
Gold Coast Music Industry Association	An organisation that facilitates local festivals, music conferences and workshops, and development initiatives to its membership of Gold Coast-based musicians.	This co-operative alliance was initiated by the Gold Coast City Council in an effort to increase the interaction between community organisations.	Benefits included presenting new opportunities to cross-publicise festival events via established e-mail channels. Additionally, the film festival was able to utilise music supplied by the association's members as part of its pre-show entertainment. The use of this music not only provided GCFF with royalty-free music tracks, but also increased the audience size as the musicians and their families and friends often attended screenings to hear their songs played.

Gold Coast Bazaar	An annual month-long celebration of fashion, food and fun hosted by Gold Coast Tourism.	This co-operative alliance was an opportunity for GCFF to raise its profile among the Gold Coast community and co-ordinate the first 'Fantastic Sneak Peek'. The 'Fantastic Sneak Peek' was a one-off, pre-release screening of a commercial film.	Through this co-operative alliance, GCFF was able to successfully introduce and test the participant acceptance of the 'Fantastic Sneak Peek' concept with very little possibility of financial or participation-driven entropy. Similarly, the fact that the screened film ensured the involvement of the local film industry meant the festival director could contact those individuals previously disillusioned with GCFF and invite them as guests to the event. The result was a re-energisation of particular film industry members and the promise of further future interaction.
Riding for the Disabled Association	A voluntary, non-profit organisation that provides opportunities for anyone with a disability to enjoy safe, healthy, stimulating, therapeutic, horse-related activities in Australia.	The co-operative alliance was based upon an interactive media project facilitated by the film festival titled 'Possibilities'.	The alliance enabled GCFF to apply for Festivals Australia funding and also represented a new demographic of participants, both through the involvement of attendance by members and participants in the 'Possibilities' project. Also, it validated the functional role of GCFF as a facilitator of activities involving youth and new media. Such an alliance also served as a socially responsible example of good citizenship.
SISCO	An arts-based youth organisation.	The co-operative alliance with SISCO presented an opportunity to publicise GCFF to schools and interested students via the SISCO network.	The benefit of this partnership was the insider access afforded to GCFF to raise awareness of the film festival.

increase its potential access to a wider choice of venues, as the festival would not conflict with what was known to be a busy box office period for Gold Coast cinemas. Similarly, the scheduling of the event prior to these major sporting events enabled the festival to take advantage of the heightened sporting atmosphere in the region; an atmosphere that, it was hoped, would also raise awareness of the festival itself.

Location

The Gold Coast is an ideal physical setting to host a film festival; the climate and geography conspire to make the region an ideal place for just about anything other than snow skiing. There was little to be done to enhance the attractiveness of the event with regards to the surrounding environment. Yet insofar as the actual location of the festival was concerned, the decision was made to hold the festival at a multiplex located at the Pacific Fair Shopping Centre, considered to be 'a Gold Coast landmark' and 'one of Australia's most iconic shopping centres' (Gold Coast 2009). The Gold Coast is a sprawling city, yet the positioning of the festival at this particular location contributed to a sense of the event lying at the city's heart. The shopping centre is also located along the Gold Coast Highway and features the main public transport interchange for the southern Gold Coast.

The cinema itself featured a large foyer throughout which displays and GCFF signage could be posted. Similarly, the theatres utilised by the GCFF were modest in size at just over 200 seats and thus allowed for mid-sized audiences to attend the screenings. The decision to hold the GCFF at a movie complex in one of Australia's largest shopping centres was not as beneficial as it could have been as, mystifyingly, the management of Pacific Fair would not endorse the film festival. Though the location was certainly not detrimental to the event – it was centrally located, close to public transport and boasted lots of parking – it simply did not reach its full potential. If, on the other hand, Pacific Fair had been amenable to the forming of a co-operative alliance, the benefits of the location (in the shape of shop window displays, in-house corporate newsletters and e-mails, etc.) would have increased the exposure of the event significantly.

Identifiable function

Communication of the Gold Coast Film Fantastic purpose presented it as a film festival endeavouring to fulfil the following four functional roles:

- providing entertainment to the Gold Coast community through sports-themed, fantasy-based or locally-produced feature films;

- involving the Gold Coast filmmaking community in competition and skills-building activities through new media;

- creating an environment in which the youth of the Gold Coast could participate in numerous activities involving film, new media and sports; and

- introducing new audiences to film.

These functions were clearly communicated on GCFF sponsorship material, in public funding applications and at public speaking engagements. The aim of announcing the festival's intentions in these areas was twofold: first it was an attempt to frame the perspectives of resource providers towards the event; by defining the function of GCFF, any ambiguity about the intentions and purpose of the event was reduced. (Ironically, given that the naming of the event as the Gold Coast Film Fantastic was a deliberate ploy to draw attention away from any 'cultural' claims the festival may have had by removing any mention of a festival from the title, there was now much confusion as to what kind of an event the GFCC actually was).

The second purpose of outlining this identifiable function was to make a declaration of the functional territory that the event would occupy. That is, in order to ensure that the GCFF would have first option to import film-related resources, e.g. locally produced films, the event needed to be seen as possessing an air of authority. The ultimate goal was to develop a reverse dependency situation where participants would come to look to the festival to fulfil their personal goals and gratification, rather than for the festival to have to canvass their support. Such a state would obviously help greatly in contributing to stable and continuous operation.

This was a strategy that was also instrumental in the re-positioning of the festival as a Gold Coast community event. Although the film industry was not completely removed from the festival's attention, it was felt that the new, reduced role of the film industry within the event was much more realistic given the obvious subordinate status the GCFF enjoyed in comparison to other existing Australian film festivals.

Legitimising affiliations

Pre-existing legitimising affiliations were used in order to promote participation from new associations and relationships which were then, in turn, used to further the validity of the GCFF as an active film festival and to confirm its standing within the Gold Coast community. Interestingly, once the film festival had attained a certain number of affiliations, it became almost mandatory for other various individuals and groups to participate, simply because they did not want to risk the consequences of being left out.

Chart 2 identifies and details the legitimising affiliations employed to leverage the GCFF towards an increase in the motivation of participants.

Participation-based incentives

The GCFF 2008 offered events at a level of quality that would motivate participation: film premières, guest filmmakers, film industry-led workshops and seminars. In addition, external events were arranged via what was called Mobile Screen Fantastic, a project consisting of an outdoor cinema purchased through a grant from the Community Gambling Benefit Fund. It facilitated the possibility of fostering a year-round film culture – keeping the environment energised and cognisant of the GCFF – and provided entertainment for those community members, such as young families, not likely to attend indoor cinema screenings.

Additional gratification was offered in the form of low ticket prices (just over half the price of a standard movie ticket), the chance for interaction with established filmmakers and skills-building workshops, which were offered free of charge. Among the notable filmmakers leading these workshops were Dana and Wes Brown, the celebrated surf filmmakers who directed and produced *Step into Liquid* (Dana Brown, U.S., 2003). The Browns' involvement was to be a critical component in legitimising the event and highlighting its sports-theme.

The film festival was purposefully framed as a unique experience so as to enhance the perceived value of participation. Therefore, the media was employed as much as possible, to create within the Gold Coast community the impression that the film festival was thriving and that participation offered potential resource providers a once-in-a-lifetime experience and opportunity.

Individual sponsorship deals were struck. And lessons were learned about cause and effect, and subjectivity. One private sponsor required that a self-made 10-second advertisement be played at least six times in the pre-screening slideshow. While this seemed a reasonably benign stipulation at the time, it came to serve as an irritant to audience members who grew tired of seeing the same promotion repeated, as it were, ad nauseam.

The Gold Coast media played a major role in re-energising sponsors and funders towards renewing their participation in the event. Interviews, photos, social articles and full-page features, were all published in the months prior to the four-day film festival and during its operation. This press coverage provided the proof that money had been allocated to a meaningful community event. All press coverage was kept and recorded, and data regarding the style and readership of all publications featuring GCFF was supplied with every funding acquittal to deliberately frame the GCFF as an effective and popular event worthy of future financial contributions.

One of the more interesting aspects of this particular strategy was encountering the gatekeeper mentality of members of the media. In order to gain access to the media it was first necessary to motivate the individual reporter/journalist/radio host to participate. To accomplish this, constant pampering contact was maintained with the various media outlets, alerting said individual reporter/journalist/radio host to potential stories that might be of interest or to opportunities to interview notable festival guests. For the most part this technique worked, yet ultimately control over perceptions of the value of the festival's resources was surrendered to and contingent upon an individual journalist's decision of what was or was not newsworthy.

The effectiveness of the participation-based incentives strategy is intended to continue to grow with the further establishment of the GCFF as an organisation that has achieved a certain 'standing' in the film industry on the Gold Coast. Similarly, the versatility and range of incentives that the festival can offer to potential participants in the area could further develop the dependency certain groups have upon the festival. Awards or distribution opportunities for local films, for example, would help to strengthen the need local filmmakers have for the event and could ultimately be used to refine the strategy of resource control.

Resource control

This strategy was not as viable as others due to the sorry state of the Open System conditions encountered during re-activation. Resource control is an aspect of film festival operation that can only be established and strengthened through repeated successful operational cycles. Even so, some influence was exerted over some resources. A *Surfing – Show 'n' Tell* project saw films being entered into the film festival specifically and solely because surf filmmakers Wes and Dana Brown were critiquing the submissions. This is a neat example of a legitimising affiliation (the

Chart 2: The 2008 GCFF ligitimising affiliations

Affiliation type	Participation gained	Benefits
Organiser-based affiliation	Festival guests, volunteers, filmmakers and audience members.	The use of personal contacts meant I could call upon people for specific duties ranging from public relations to ushering. Similarly, my personal experience as a film festival director enabled me to make choices in accordance with the most beneficial timing so as to generate the best possible outcome for the event.
Organisation-based affiliation	Members of the Gold Coast film industry.	The film festival was affiliated under the recently formed Film Gold Coast, the screen production branch of the Gold Cost City Council's Economic Development and Major Projects Directorate. Film Gold Coast had a steering committee made up individuals from the local film industry, including the vice president of Studio Operations of Warner Roadshow Studios. This affiliation provided immediate access to major players in the Gold Coast film industry.
Patron/official guest-based affiliation	Audience members, media coverage and sponsorship/funding support.	As the official patron of GCFF, John Cox's presence was useful with regard to the opportunity for media exposure and for the letters of endorsement he provided which were regularly included in funding submissions. Guest filmmakers such as Dana and Wes Brown (Step into Liquid, Dana Brown, U.S., 2003) proved irresistible to surfing fans as they hosted question and answer sessions and participated in a wildly popular Surfing - Show 'n'Tell.
Board of directors-based affiliation	Sponsorship and audience members.	The services of a local law office were arranged pro bono through a board member's employer. Similarly, a professional makeup artist also serving as a board member provided valuable services by facilitating a make-up workshop that attracted the participation of those interested in a career in theatrical/film make-up.

Sponsor-based affiliation	Sponsorship/funding support	Gold Coast City Council was the first sponsor approached by GCFF and its participation was viewed as critical due to its position as the regional government authority. Once sponsorship was confirmed a series of second-tier government sponsors were contacted such as the Community Gambling Benefit Fund at the State level, and Festivals Australia at the Federal level.
		Community Gambling Benefit Fund sponsorship was used to facilitate the 'Mobile Screen Fantastic'. Through this traveling film festival several strategic co-operative alliances were entered into, increasing the presence and social connectivity of the event.
		Festivals Australia provided the funding for the 'Possibilities' expanded cinema project and enabled co-operative alliances with Riding for the Disabled while also increasing the cultural worth and prestige of the festival.
		The Pacific Film and Television Commission was applied to last. Only when funding from Festivals Australia, the Community Gambling Benefit Fund and Gold Coast City Council was confirmed did GCFF a present a submission. This was a successful tactic and funding from PFTC was granted. This funding was instrumental in providing unrestricted monies for project development and operational costs.
		The festival also undertook to engage a number of private sponsors, including a Gold Coast-based Brewery, a local law firm and a commercial printer. The participation of these private businesses helped the festival through in-kind services and some minor financial contributions.

presence of the Browns) conspiring with a participation-based incentive (being judged by the Browns) to work to the distinct advantage of the festival. Oddly enough, it was even possible to exercise a form of 'resource control' over the Browns: as part of the agreement to secure their involvement, the two filmmakers were to provide the festival with a previously unseen, twenty-minute edit of their soon to be released film *Highwater* (Dana Brown, U.S., 2009).

Additional resource control was developed with the acquisition of the portable outdoor cinema, the Mobile Screen Fantastic. Owning this equipment meant that the film festival could facilitate screenings in all sorts of places and with only basic logistical considerations, e.g. power, space, etc. Control of this resource meant that the GCFF would no longer be dependent upon commercial theatres as its only means of showing films.

Sanctioning organisations

Two sanctioning organisations were identified as being able to provide the GCFF with greater access to the resources it required. The festival had been positioned as a hybrid sports-themed fantasy film festival and required a sheltering umbrella of approval from organisations involved with each of these social worlds. The challenge of gaining any affiliation with sanctioning organisations is that ultimately they must select the festival for inclusion. That is, a particular film festival must fit accord with the sanctioning organisation's overall goals, and so a protracted application process of evaluation of possible candidates must be entered into.

Sports Business Taskforce (SBT) is 'an industry-based body that undertakes promotion, marketing and networking to attract sports business to Gold Coast City'. The SBT's vision for the city as 'a premier sports destination and world-class supplier of sport goods and services' (Business GC 2009) made it instantly recognisable as a sanctioning organisation whose affiliation would be important in helping the GCFF establish and promote its sports film theme. Because ninety per cent of the region's sporting business offices are locally situated, the sanctioning of the SBT was a valuable means for gaining both legitimacy in and access to that particular pool of resources. In fact, GCFF was able to screen trailers of upcoming films programmed into the festival at the SBT quarterly meetings and it was through SBT that GCFF was able to first make contact with the Burleigh Brewing Company, a company that would later sponsor several of the GCFF sports-themed events and be a provider of liquid gratification to more than a handful of audience participants.

Equally as enticing was the opportunity to be affiliated with a number of important fantasy-based film festivals, such as the Belgium-based International Fantastic Film Festival (BIFFF), the Puchon International Fantastic Film Festival, and the Fantasia International Film Festival (www.fantasiafestival.com) in Canada. The European Fantastic Film Festivals Federation (EFFFF) was contacted regarding membership so as to help develop possible additional programming channels to those presented by Australian distributors. The EFFFF is a film festival sanctioning body based in Brussels. It represents 20 festivals in Europe, Asia and North America and claims that with

> a joint audience of approximately 600,000 spectators, the European Fantastic Film Festivals Federation has become one of the most powerful tools to promote the originality and creativity of the European fantasy film industry. (EFFFF 2009)

Membership of EFFFF would aim to address problems of operations-driven entropy. The fact that the GCFF was specialising in fantasy films meant that it was dependent upon a niche market. To make matters more challenging, the festival only acquired fantasy films via Australian distributors, thus its programme was doubly dependent on a limited resource. In order to gain entry into the federation, proof of viable operation by the GCFF was required in the form of documentation demonstrating the strength of the festival's programme, listings of any patrons or important guest filmmakers involved and detailing workshops or other sidebar activities. After having prepared and presented this information, I was informed that the GCFF's membership would not be decided on until the next general assembly, which coincided with Cannes and so, unfortunately, even if successful, this strategy would not be implemented until the following operational cycle.

However, membership into EFFFF was not without its drawbacks. Joining the federation is not free of charge and in order to become a full member, the GCFF would have been required to host another EFFFF member at the festival. Thus, there were economic considerations connected to this strategy. Membership could also pose an operational challenge if the EFFFF decided not to permit the GCFF to screen sports films by perceiving a conflict with the federation's fantasy image.

These matters were left for consideration by future GCFF organisers who would make decisions regarding the Open System strengths of the GCFF as a hybrid fantasy/sports-themed event. Alternatively, by utilising the new benefits offered by EFFFF membership, such as increased fantasy film supply, membership into an established festival network, and an increased chance of greater fantasy film industry participation, the GCFF could see itself undergoing another change of form and function and reverting to its previous incarnation as a site for more specialised fantasy film exhibition.

The deployment of these eight strategies sparked the Gold Coast Film Fantastic into a new age of being. Gone were the old notions of a monolithic event bent on world domination. Instead, the Gold Coast had a film festival, created through community partnerships and mutually beneficial participation. The event had its flaws and in its hybrid sports/ fantasy form was idiosyncratic, but the effects of the re-energisation and the gratification experienced by key participants carved out a foothold from which subsequent Film Fantastics could continue advancing.

My role as the Gold Coast Film Fantastic festival director lasted only 14 months and, for the most part, that directorship period was concerned with the re-activation or finding of new resources that could sustain the event. During the 10-month lead-up to the festival I was able to secure over AUD$120,000 [US$114,000] in funding and in-kind contributions totalling close to AUD$115,000 [US$109,000].

The money was nice but from an Open System Paradigm perspective the most important achievement was the resultant social connectivity. The community, film industry and local government now knew that the Film Fantastic existed and performed particular roles within the Gold Coast region. Whether it was as a source of community entertainment, as a facilitator of skill-building activities for filmmakers, as a provider of opportunities for youth to engage with new media or as a supplier of film culture, various participants now looked to the GCFF as a vehicle to advance their own goals and agendas.

In 2012 the Gold Coast Film Fantastic – now the Gold Coast Film Festival (www.gcfilmfestival.com) – is a vibrant and thriving event. The organisers continue to develop co-operative alliances, forming partnerships with prominent organisations such as the Asian Screen Pacific Awards (APSA) (www.asiapacificscreenacademy.com), and they have expanded the festival's contact base through legitimising affiliations with high-level government officials. By all accounts the event has made a full recovery and has a clean bill of health for the foreseeable future.

As for myself, a few months after the GCFF I was recruited into a management position at the Brisbane International Film Festival, a larger, more established event that gave me greater scope to examine film festival operation through my then still-evolving conceptualisation of the Open System Paradigm. The victories and losses I experienced while at Brisbane proved to me that film festival management is as much about overcoming adversity as is it about screening films, the key being to know how to read situations and position the event for the best possible outcome.

Conclusion: Done and Dusted

On 29 March, 2012 *Variety Online* announced that Latvia's International Film Festival Arsenals (www.arsenals.lv/) would no longer continue. After a quarter of a century of operation 'one of Eastern Europe's oldest film festivals' was forced into retirement due to a lack of funding (Holdsworth 2012). Case closed on another unique festival.

There is something familiar about this story. The inability of Arsenals' organisers to reach 'a trilateral co-operation agreement between Riga City Council and Culture Ministry' ('How to Organize a Film Festival' 2012) reflects the lack of success in forming co-operative alliances or legitimizing affiliations with major purse string holders. It is also a consequence of the reported difficulties that resulted from 'frequent changes' in the festival directorship that ultimately led to a 'weakening of the event's international profile' (Holdsworth 2012). This is a revolving door leadership situation reminiscent of the case study of the Gold Coast Film Fantastic. Additionally, there is the appearance of the Black Knight, Estonia's Tallinn Black Night Film Festival (2012.poff. ee/eng), which over the past 16 years continued to steal Arsenals' Baltic spotlight and with it the majority of film industry participants (Ibid.).

So was it merely a lack of funding that led this veteran film festival to the grave? Yes and no. The film festival had money. In fact, the Cultural Ministry had given the festival organisers the equivalent of US$30,000 for the 2012 event, an increase of US $11,000 from 2011 (Holdsworth 2012). Similarly, the Riga City Council publically announced a contribution of 'nearly $35,000' to the 2012 event (Ibid.). A financial total of nearly US$65,000 in sponsorship money from two participants is not too shabby given the current economic climate. But what about 2013?

Could it be that Arsenals' organisers saw the writing on the wall and deliberately scuttled their festival to prove a point? Behind closed governmental doors the viability of the event was being questioned and the 2012 payoffs represented both a parting gift and the last chance for festival organisers to prove themselves and gratify their benefactors. Interestingly, an on-line petition instituted by Arsenals' organisers explicitly bemoaned the 'short-sighted' nature of cutting future cultural funding and called the attention of other festival participants to the dangerous mindset of 'the government of Latvia, the Ministry of Culture and the Riga City Council' (Arsenals 2012). This reflects a complex issue of collective identity and perhaps the appearance of a hybrid resource control strategy that involves shaming one participant group for endangering the existence of the film festival – such is the paradox of social system organisations.

This book is meant to help film festival organisers make sense of the complex, contradictory and unforgiving environment that social system organisations, such as the festival they are organising, occupy. From the first example to the last, the situations presented here are intended to demonstrate the need to examine an event beyond its headlines so as to understand the intricacies of film festival operation and ultimately grasp what truly makes these events tick.

The management concepts discussed here are not new or revolutionary. The Greeks proposed and practiced system-based thought over 2,000 years ago: it is fitting that ideas from the civilization that defined so much of our dramatic arts should become the basis for understanding one of the most prolific exhibitory events in human history. The Open System Paradigm offers the apparent simplicity necessary to effectively operate a film festival in a complicated world. The four phases of basic operation are not only logical but also easy to communicate – an important aspect when it comes to convincing those people essential to operation, whether they are board members, sponsors or the reluctant artist of the advantages and dangers of their involvement.

Interestingly, on the very same day that Arsenals was pronounced dead the small African nation of Sierra Leone held its first international film festival, the aptly named Sierra Leone International Film Festival (www.sierraleoneinternationalfilmfestival.com). Of course, the future of this event is as unpredictable as that of any start up festival, but its very existence does give a sense of vindication and hope. Regardless of any apparent adversity, there is always the possibility that the environment is right for film festival organisers to create and develop sustainable projections of their own

Notes

1   This figure was reached by typing in the term 'film festival' into the Google search engine on 25 June 2011.

2   The location of many film festivals is not always discernable by their titles. Some events, such as Cannes, are immediately recognisable to those with the most basic knowledge of the existence of film festivals. Others, however, require signposting so as to give the reader a reference to the geographical location being discussed.

3   Peranson's distinction between business and audience focused film festivals raises interesting issues with regard to the functional role of film festivals. A thought-provoking alternative to this dualist model is provided in the doctoral thesis by Tit Leung Cheung (2012) which posits a much broader range of motives behind many East-Asian documentary film festivals in particular – from cultural and educational to archival and developmental imperatives, where some of the festivals reaffirm the importance of filmmakers, which are accounted as the least important among the interest groups of Peranson's model. There is no one-size-fits-all when it comes to film festivals.

4   The SECOR Consulting analysis was commissioned by Telefilm Canada and the Québec-based cultural funding agency, Société de Développement des Entreprises Culturelles (SODEC) as a means of assessing the operational capacities of the four major Canadian film festivals. The Canadian film festivals included in this study are: The Toronto International Film Festival (tiff.net), the World Film Festival (Montréal) (www.ffm-montreal.org/), the Vancouver International Film Festival (www.viff.org), and the Atlantic Film Festival (www.atlanticfilm.com).

5   Marijke de Valck argues that a film festival is an 'obligatory point of passage' and 'vital and important' to the flow (production, distribution, and consumption) of film within the cinema network.

6   It is common for a film to travel from one film festival to another, effectively touring what is known as the film festival circuit. The transactions of the film festival circuit are also indicative of a larger, global system which links film festivals together. More information about the film festival circuit can be found in *Film Festival Yearbook 1: The Festival Circuit* (2009).

7   The complete list of Open System characteristics identified by Katz and Kahn are: (1) importation of energy, (2) the throughput of energy, (3) the output of energy, (4) systems as cycles of events, (5) negative entropy, (6) information input, negative feedback and the coding process, (7) the steady state and dynamic homeostasis, (8) differentiation, (9) integration and coordination, (10) equifinality. For more information, see: Katz, Daniel and Robert L. Kahn (1978) *The Social Psychology of Organizations.*

8   Lulls in operational expenditure as well as large influxes of resources into an event can be seen to stop-up entropic leaks, thus enabling film festival organisers to begin each film festival with a 'full bucket'.

9   Marijke de Valck notes that the estimated number of film festivals currently operating worldwide each year lies between 1,200 and 1,900 (2007: 68).

10   In 2011 the Pusan International Film Festival officially became the Busan International Film Festival. For more information about this name change go to the festival's webpage on: http://busanhaps.com/article/biff/piff-becomes-biff.

11   The connection between De Niro and Tribeca is so strong that the film festival has been referred to as 'Robert De Niro's Film Festival' (Softpedia 2006).

12   For a very interesting take on the social function of awards as cultural validators see James English (2005) *Economy of Prestige: Prizes, Awards, and the Circulation of Cultural Value.*

13   The political unrest in Egypt during 2011 saw the first suspension of the Cairo International Film Festival. Interestingly, FIAPF assured Cairo's organisers that the event would not be 'relegated to a lower status' and that no other country would 'hold the festival in Cairo's place' (Hosni 2011).

14   The Warner Roadshow Studios opened on the Gold Coast in 1991 (Google 2009).

15   Ironically, the Gold Coast Film Fantastic changed its name to the Gold Coast Film Festival in 2010.

16   Frampton would withdraw his support for the event in 2005 after becoming disillusioned with his supervisory role in the festival.

Bibliography

48-Hour Film Project (2010) 'Official Rules', *48-Hour Film Project*. On-line. Available HTTP: http://www.48hourfilm.com/filmmakers/rules-official.php (24 September 2012).

Alexander, Craig (1997) 'Dragons and Tigers take on Leopards and Skunks: The Importance of Film Festivals', *Performing Arts & Entertainment in Canada*, 31, 2, 16-17.

Amdur, Meredith and David Rooney (2004) 'Preem Dreams in Tribeca', *Variety*. On-line. Available HTTP: http://www.variety.com/article/VR1117901219.html (24 September 2012).

Art Film Fest (2009) 'Record Attendance at Art Film Fest', *Artfilmfest.com*. On-line. Available HTTP: http://www.artfilmfest.sk/en/press/press-releases/press/record-attendance-at-art-film-fest/2b0c3ab435/ (31 March 2012).

Australian Film Institute (2009) 'About AFI', *The Australian Film Institute*. On-line. Available HTTP: http://www.afi.org.au/AM/ContentManagerNet/HTMLDisplay.aspx?ContentID=8836&Section=About (24 September 2012).

Bangré, Sambolgo (1996) 'African Cinema in the Tempest of Minor Festivals', in Imruh Bakari and Mbye Cham (eds) *African Experiences in Cinema*. London: British Film Institute, 157-61.

Barraclough, Leo (2004) 'Scott, Breillat to Lead Berlin Sessions', *Variety*. On-line. Available HTTP: http://www.variety.com/article/VR1117915260.html?categoryid=1061&cs=1 (24 September 2012).

Beauchamp, Cari and Henri Béhar (1992) *Hollywood on the Riviera: The Inside Story of the Cannes Film Festival*. New York: William Morrow and Company.

Benson, Sheila (1998) 'Mill Valley Film Festival (20th)', in Steven Gaydos (ed) *The Variety Guide to Film Festivals: The Ultimate Insider's Guide to Film Festivals Around the World*. New York: Berkley Publishing Group, 147-9.

Berlin Film Festival (2009a) 'Berlin Film Festival', *Berlinale*. On-line. Available HTTP: http://www.berlinale.de/en/HomePage.html (17 October 2011).

Berlin Film Festival (2009b) 'WCF Profile', *Berlinale*. On-line. Available HTTP: http://www.berlinale.de/en/das_festival/world_cinema_ fund/wcf_profil/index.html (26 November 2011).

Birchenough, Tom (2005) 'Moscow Fest Picks Jury', *Variety*. On-line. Available HTTP: http://www.variety.com/article/VR1117923971. html (24 September 2012).

Biskind, Peter (2004) *Down and Dirty Pictures: Miramax, Sundance and the Rise of Independent Film*. New York: Simon & Schuster Paperbacks.

Boland, Michaela (2009) 'Loach pulls "Eric" from Melbourne', *Variety*. On-line. Available HTTP: http://www.variety.com/article/ VR1118006192.html?categoryid=13&cs=1&nid=2597 (24 September 2012).

Boulding, Kenneth (1956) 'General Systems Theory: The Skeleton of Science', *Management Science*, 2, 3, 197-208.

Bowser, Kathryn (2009) 'Working with Filmmakers', interview by L. Tanner, in Tanner, Lauri Rose (ed) (2009) *Creating Film Festivals: Everything You Wanted to Know but Didn't Know Who to Ask*. Oakland: Lauri Rose Tanner, 140.

Box Office Network (2009) 'International Film Festival Summit Announces Faculty for the Certified Film Festival Professional Program', *Box Office Network*. On-line. Available HTTP: http:// boxofficenewsreport.com/a683250-international-film-festival-summit-announces-faculty.cfm (15 October 2011).

Brown, William (2009) 'The Festival Syndrome', in Dina Iordanova and
Ragan Rhyne (eds) *Film Festival Yearbook 1: The Festival Circuit*. St.
Andrews: St Andrews Film Studies with College Gate Press, 216-25.

Burton, Natasha (2005) 'Slamdance Calls for Entries', *Variety*. On-line.
Available HTTP: http://www.variety.com/article/VR1117925598.
html (24 September 2012).

Canadian Broadcasting Corporation (2009) 'Loach Pulls Melbourne
Festival Film in Israeli Funding Protest', *CBC News*. On-line.
Available HTTP: http://www.cbc.ca/arts/film/story/2009/07/20/
loach-israel.html (24 September 2012).

Cantrell, Lorena (2009) Interview by L. Tanner, in Tanner, Lauri Rose (ed)
(2009) *Creating Film Festivals: Everything You Wanted to Know but
Didn't Know Who to Ask*. Oakland: Lauri Rose Tanner, 114-121.

Cheung, Ruby (2009) 'Corporatising a Film Festival: Hong Kong', in Dina
Iordanova and Ragan Rhyne (eds) *Film Festival Yearbook 1: The
Festival Circuit*. St. Andrews: St Andrews Film Studies with College
Gate Press, 99-115.

Cheung, Ruby (2010) 'We Believe in "Film as Art" An Interview with Li
Cheuk-to, Artistic Director of the Hong Kong International Film
Festival', in Dina Iordanova and Ruby Cheung (eds) *Film Festival
Yearbook 3: Film Festivals and East Asia*. St Andrews: St Andrews
Film Studies, 196-207.

Cheung, Tit Leung (2012) *Extending the Local: Documentary Film
Festivals in East Asia as Sites of Connection and Communication*.
Unpublished PhD Thesis. Hong Kong: Lingnan University,
Department of Visual Studies.

Cousins, Mark (2009) 'Widescreen on Film Festivals', in Dina Iordanova
and Ragan Rhyne (eds) *Film Festival Yearbook 1: The Festival Circuit*.
St. Andrews: St Andrews Film Studies with College Gate Press,
155-158.

Cowie, Peter (ed) (2002) *Variety International Film Guide 2002*. London: Faber & Faber.

Cowie, Peter (ed) (2003) *Variety International Film Guide 2003*. London: Faber & Faber.

Crawford, Peter Ian and David Turton (eds) (1992) *Film as Ethnography*. Manchester: Manchester University Press.

Daft, Richard L. (1997) *Management*. Fort Worth: Dryden Press.

Daft, Richard L. and Mark P. Sharfman (1990) *Organization Theory: Cases and Applications*. St. Paul: West Publishing Company.

Dawes, Amy (1993) 'Chief Out at Palm Springs Film Fest', *Los Angeles Times*. On-line. Available HTTP: http://articles.latimes.com/1993-08-03/entertainment/ca-19817_1_palm-springs-international-film-festival (24 September 2012).

de La Fuente, Anna Marie (2004) 'Venice Fest Will Have an American Accent', *Variety*. On-line. Available HTTP: http://www.variety.com/article/VR1117902002.html?categoryid=1611&cs=1 (24 September 2012).

de La Fuente, Anna Marie (2006) 'L.A. Latino Fest Slates Gabi Nod for Banderas', *Variety*. On-line. Available HTTP: http://www.variety.com/article/VR1117951124.html (24 September 2012).

de Valck, Marijke (2007) *Film Festivals: From European Geopolitics to Global Cinephilia*. Amsterdam: Amsterdam University Press.

de Valck, Marijke and Skadi Loist (2008) 'Thematic, Annotated Bibliography. Second Edition', *Film Festival Research*. On-line. Available HTTP: http://www1.uni-hamburg.de/Medien/berichte/arbeiten/0091_08.html (24 September 2012).

de Valck, Marijke and Skadi Loist (2009) 'Film Festival Studies: An Overview of a Burgeoning Field', in Dina Iordanova and Ragan Rhyne (eds) *Film Festival Yearbook 1: The Festival Circuit*. St. Andrews: St Andrews Film Studies with College Gate Press, 179-215.

Deauville American Film Festival (2012) 'History', *Deauville American Film Festival website*. On-line. Available HTTP: http://www.festival-deauville.com/DEV/index.php?pid=49 (24 September 2012).

Di Mara, Tom (2009) 'Starting Festivals', interview by L. Tanner, in Tanner, Lauri Rose (ed) (2009) *Creating Film Festivals: Everything You Wanted to Know but Didn't Know Who to Ask*. Oakland: Lauri Rose Tanner, 132.

DiCaprio, Leonardo (1999) 'Features: Leofest'. Online. Available HTTP: http://dicapriocom.free.fr/features/leofest.php

DiMaggio, Paul and Walter Powell (1988) 'The Iron Cage Revisited: Institutional Isomorphism and Collective Rationality in Organizational Fields', in Carl Milofsky (ed) *Community Organizations*. New York: Oxford University Press, 77-99.

Eldridge, Pippa and Julia Voss (2010) *How to Set Up a Film Festival*. British Film Institute. Online. Available HTTP: http://www.bfi.org.uk/sites/bfi.org.uk/files/downloads/bfi-how-to-set-up-a-film-festival-2001.pdf (31 March 2012).

Elley, Derek and Jon Hopewell (1998) 'Locarno International Film Festival (51st)', in Steven Gaydos (ed) *The Variety Guide to Film Festivals: The Ultimate Insider's Guide to Film Festivals Around the World*. New York: Berkley Publishing Group, 113-114.

Elley, Derek and Jon Hopewell (2004) '"Private" Pulls Locarno Rank', *Variety*. On-line. Available HTTP: http://www.variety.com/article/VR1117909091?refCatId=1236 (24 September 2012).

Elley, Derek and Jon Hopewell (2005) 'Pusan Fest Plans Fireworks', *Variety*. On-line. Available HTTP: http://www.variety.com/article/VR1117924158.html (24 September 2012).

Elley, Derek and Jon Hopewell (2007) 'Cannes Fest Ups Thierry Frémaux', *Variety*. On-line. Available HTTP: http://www.variety.com/article/VR1117970951.html (24 September 2012).

Elsner-Sommer, Gretchen (2009) Interview by L. Tanner, in Tanner, Lauri Rose (ed) (2009) *Creating Film Festivals: Everything You Wanted to Know but Didn't Know Who to Ask*. Oakland: Lauri Rose Tanner, 97-101.

English, James F. (2005) *The Economy of Prestige: Prizes, Awards, and the Circulation of Cultural Value*. London: Harvard University Press.

European Coordination of Film Festivals (no date) 'Introduction', European Coordination of Film Festivals website. On-line. Available HTTP: http://www.femmetotale.de/z_pages/ecff_e.html (24 September 2012).

European Fantastic Film Festivals Federation (2009) 'European Fantastic Film Festivals Federation', *Méliès d'Or website*. On-line. Available HTTP: http://www.melies.org/ (24 September 2012).

Fallaux, Emile (2009) Interview by L. Tanner, in Tanner, Lauri Rose (ed) (2009) *Creating Film Festivals: Everything You Wanted to Know but Didn't Know Who to Ask*. Oakland: Lauri Rose Tanner, 51-61.

Fédération Internationale de la Presse Cinématographique (FIPRESCI) (2009) *Statutes*. On-line. Available HTTP: http://www.fipresci.org/about/statutes.htm (24 September 2012).

Fédération Internationale des Associations de Producteurs de Films (FIAPF) (2010) *International Film Festivals*. On-line. Available HTTP: http://www.fiapf.org/intfilmfestivals.asp (24 September 2012).

Field, Simon (2009) 'The Sandwich Process: Simon Field Talks about Polemics and Poetry at Film Festivals'. Interview by James Quandt, in Richard Porton (ed.) *Dekalog 3: On Film Festivals*. London: Wallflower Press, 53-80.

Film Festival World (2008) 'Film Festival World', *filmfestivalworld.com*. On-line. Available HTTP: http://www.filmfestivalworld.com/ (31 March 2012).

Film Festival World (2010) 'Academies & Awards – An FFW Resource', *filmfestivalworld.com*. On-line. Available HTTP: http://www. filmfestivalworld.com/resources/#rsrc35 (24 September 2012).

Fishkin, Mark (2009a) 'It's a Hard Road… You Don't Get Into it for the Money', interview by L. Tanner, in Tanner, Lauri Rose (ed.) (2009) *Creating Film Festivals: Everything You Wanted to Know but Didn't Know Who to Ask*. Oakland: Lauri Rose , 23-24.

Fishkin, Mark (2009b) 'There has to be a Need', interview by L. Tanner, in Tanner, Lauri Rose (ed.) (2009) *Creating Film Festivals: Everything You Wanted to Know but Didn't Know Who to Ask*. Oakland: Lauri Rose Tanner, 20.

Fishkin, Mark (2009c) 'You Have to Constantly Re-evaluate what is Important', interview by L. Tanner, in Tanner, Lauri Rose (ed.) (2009) *Creating Film Festivals: Everything You Wanted to Know but Didn't Know Who to Ask*. Oakland: Lauri Rose Tanner, 26-27.

Flickerfest (2009) '2010 Entry Form', *Flickerfest*. On-line. Available HTTP: http://entryform2010.flickerfest.com.au/index.php/entry/new (24 September 2012).

Fox, Michael (2009) 'Film Covers the Whole Universe', interview by L. Tanner, in Tanner, Lauri Rose (ed.) (2009) *Creating Film Festivals: Everything You Wanted to Know but Didn't Know Who to Ask*. Oakland: Lauri Rose Tanner, 146-153.

Franey, Alan (2009) Interview by L. Tanner, in Tanner, Lauri Rose (ed.) (2009) *Creating Film Festivals: Everything You Wanted to Know but Didn't Know Who to Ask*. Oakland: Lauri Rose Tanner, 28-32.

Frater, Patrick (2005) 'Skip City Digital Fest Unspools in Sapporo', *Variety*. On-line. Available HTTP: http://www.variety.com/article/ VR1117926052.html (24 September 2012).

Frater, Patrick (2006) 'Beyond Borders', *Variety*. On-line. Available HTTP: http://www.variety.com/article/VR1117951695.html (24 September 2012).

Galaskiewicz, Joseph and Barbara Rauschenbach (1988) 'The Corporation-Culture Connection: A Test of Interorganizational Theories', in Carl Milofsky (ed.) *Community Organizations. Studies in Resource Mobilization and Exchange.* New York: Oxford University Press, 119-35.

Gamson, Joshua (1996) 'The Organizational Shaping of Collective Identity: The Case of Lesbian and Gay Film Festivals in New York', *Sociological Forum,* 11, 2, 30.

Garcelon, Annie (2005) 'The Charitable Cursor', *Variety.* On-line. Available HTTP: http://www.variety.com/article/VR1117934729. html?categoryid=2031&cs=1 (24 September 2012).

Gavrilova, Masha (2009) 'On The Island With Aleksandr Rodnyansky', *action! Berlinale Special Edition.* Online. Available HTTP: http:// www.action-magazine.ru/images/arhive/ab2009.pdf (24 September 2012).

Gaydos, Steven (ed.) (1998a) *The Variety Guide to Film Festivals: An Insider's Guide to Film Festivals Around the World* (1st ed.). New York: Berkley Publishing Group.

Gaydos, Steven (ed.) (2005) 'Ex-Venice Topper Annexes Montreal Gig', *Variety.* On-line. Available HTTP: http://www.variety.com/article/ VR1117917653.html (24 September 2012).

Gaydos, Steven and Derek Elley (2003) 'Battle Behind the Scenes', *Variety.* On-line. Available HTTP: http://www.variety.com/article/ VR1117891416 (24 September 2012).

Getz, Donald (2007) *Event Studies: Theory, Research and Policy for Planned Events.* Oxford: Butterworth-Heinemann.

Gilmore, Geoff (2009) 'Evolution v. Revolution, the State of Independent Film & Festivals', *indiewire.com.* On-line. Available HTTP: http:// www.indiewire.com/article/first_person/ (24 September 2012).

Gilmore, Geoffrey (2009) Interview by L. Tanner, in Tanner, Lauri Rose (ed.). (2009) *Creating Film Festivals: Everything You Wanted to Know but Didn't Know Who to Ask*. Oakland: Lauri Rose Tanner, 135-137.

Globe Entertainment (2000) *Business Plan. The Gold Coast Film Event: Interim Report*. Brisbane: Gold Coast Film Fantastic. Available upon request: Gold Coast City Council.

Gold Coast (2009) 'Shopping & Markets', *Goldcoast.com.au*. On-line. Available HTTP: http://www.goldcoast.com.au/gold-coast-shopping-markets.html (26 November 2011).

Gold Coast City Council (2006) 'Gold Coast Business Survey: Sport 2006', *Gold Coast City Council website*. On-line. Available HTTP: http://www.goldcoast.qld.gov.au/attachment/EDMP/GCBS_Sport_2006.pdf (24 September 2012).

Google (2009) 'Warner Roadshow Studios Timeline', *Google.com*. On-line. Available HTTP: http://www.google.com/search?q=warner+roadshow+studios&hl=en&rls=com.microsoft:en-US&sa=X&tbo=p&tbs=tl:1,tll:1991/01,tlh:1991/12&ei=3HIQS_DhHZTs7APhnf3YBQ&oi=timeline_histogram_main&ct=timeline-histogram&cd=2&ved=0CBQQyQEoAg (31 March 2012 – broken URL).

Gore, Chris (2001) *The Ultimate Film Festival Survival Guide* (2nd ed.). Hollywood: Lone Eagle Publishing Company.

Graydon, Danny (2004) '"Nobody" Tops Flanders Fest', *Variety*. On-line. Available HTTP: http://www.variety.com/article/VR1117912079.html?categoryid=1061&cs=1 (24 September 2012).

Grey, Tobias (2006) 'Upstart Aspirations', *Variety*. On-line. Available HTTP: http://www.variety.com/article/VR1117950511.html (24 September 2012).

Haaretz Service, 'Edinburgh Film Festival Refuses Israeli Grant Due to Pressure by Ken Loach' (2009) *Haaretz.com*. On-line. Available HTTP: http://www.haaretz.com/news/edinburgh-film-festival-refuses-israeli-grant-due-to-pressure-by-ken-loach-1.276384 (24 September 2012).

Haberski, Raymond J. (2001) *It's Only a Movie!* Kentucky: The University Press of Kentucky.

Hamid, Rahul (2009) 'From Urban Bohemia to Euro Glamour: The Establishment and Early Years of The New York Film Festival', in Dina Iordanova and Ragan Rhyne (eds) *Film Festival Yearbook 1: The Festival Circuit*. St. Andrews: St Andrews Film Studies with College Gate Press, 67-80.

Harbord, Janet (2009) 'Film Festivals – Time-Event', in Dina Iordanova and Ragan Rhyne (eds) *Film Festival Yearbook 1: The Festival Circuit*. St. Andrews: St Andrews Film Studies with College Gate Press, 40-6.

Harris, Dana (2004a) 'Fests Test if Pix Click', *Variety*. On-line. Available HTTP: http:www.variety.com/article/VR1117910573.html (24 September 2012).

Harris, Dana (2004b) 'Focus on Films in Austin', *Variety*. On-line. Available HTTP: http://www.variety.com/article/VR1117901675.html?categoryid=13&cs=1 (24 September 2012).

Harris, Dana (2004c) 'Shorts Suit Palm Springs', *Variety*. On-line. Available HTTP: http://www.variety.com/article/VR1117909281.html (24 September 2012).

Harris, Dana (2005) 'Fest Beset by Party Monster', *Variety*. On-line. Available HTTP: http://www.variety.com/article/VR1117916857.html?categoryid=1238&cs=1 (24 September 2012).

Harris, Dana and Brendan Kelly (2004) 'Toronto Plays (Very) Nice', *Variety*. On-line. Available HTTP: http://www.variety.com/article/VR1117910292.html?categoryid=19&cs=1 (24 September 2012).

Hawk, Bob (2009) Interview by L. Tanner, in Tanner, Lauri Rose (ed.) (2009) *Creating Film Festivals: Everything You Wanted to Know but Didn't Know Who to Ask*. Oakland: Lauri Rose Tanner, 62-64.

Henderson, Ron (2009) Interview by L. Tanner, in Tanner, Lauri Rose (ed.) (2009) *Creating Film Festivals: Everything You Wanted to Know but Didn't Know Who to Ask*. Oakland: Lauri Rose Tanner, 122-126.

Hendrix, Grady (2005) 'So, You Want to Start a Film Festival...DON'T', *Slate.com*. On-line. Available HTTP: http://www.slate.com/articles/news_and_politics/summer_movies/2005/06/so_you_want_to_start_a_film_festival_.html (24 September 2012).

Herskovitz, Jon (1998) 'Tokyo International Film Festival (10th)', in Steven Gaydos (ed.) *The Variety Guide to Film Festivals: The Ultimate Insider's Guide to Film Festivals Around the World*. New York: Berkley Publishing Group, 166-7.

Highsted, Tim (2009) 'London and San Francisco Festivals: How to Make a Festival a "Festival" rather than just a series of Screenings', interview by L. Tanner, in Tanner, Lauri Rose (ed.) (2009) *Creating Film Festivals: Everything You Wanted to Know but Didn't Know Who to Ask*. Oakland: Lauri Rose Tanner, 37-50.

Holdsworth, Nick (2012) 'Latvia's Arsenals Film Fest Closes', *Variety*. On-line. Available HTTP: http://www.variety.com/article/VR1118052052 (24 September 2012).

Holland, Jonathan and John Hopewell (2006) 'Haute Auteurs Walk the Beach', *Variety*. On-line. Available HTTP: http://www.variety.com/article/VR1117950549.html (24 September 2012).

Hope, Cathy (2004) 'A History of the Sydney and Melbourne Film Festivals, 1945-1972: Negotiating Between Culture and Industry'. Unpublished PhD Thesis, University of Canberra, Australia.

Horne, Larry (2009) Interview by L. Tanner, in Tanner, Lauri Rose (ed.) (2009) *Creating Film Festivals: Everything You Wanted to Know but Didn't Know Who to Ask*. Oakland: Lauri Rose Tanner, 102-105.

Hosni, Mohsen (2011) 'Egyptian Film Industry Expert: Cairo Festival Will Maintain Prestige', *Arab Film Festival* website. On-line. Available HTTP: http://www.arabfilmfestival.org/wp/2011/06/06/egyptian-film-industry-expert-cairo-festival-will-maintain-prestige/ (24 September 2012).

'How to Organize a Film Festival' (2008) *eHow.com*. On-line. Available HTTP: http://www.ehow.com/how_135524_organize-film-festival.html (24 September 2012).

Huang, Yu Shan (2003) 'Creating and Distributing Films Openly: On the Relationship Between Women's Film Festivals and Women's Rights Movement in Taiwan', *Inter-Asia Cultural Studies*, 4, 1, 157-8.

Humphreys, Olivia (2011) 'How to Start a Film Festival', *Ideastapcom*. On-line. Available HTTP: http://www.ideastap.com/magazine/knowledge/how-to-start-a-film-festival (24 September 2012).

Hussey, Halfdan (2009) 'Business-World Style Success', interview by L. Tanner, in Tanner, Lauri Rose (ed.) (2009) *Creating Film Festivals: Everything You Wanted to Know but Didn't Know Who to Ask.* Oakland: Lauri Rose Tanner, 138.

International Film Festival Summit (IFFS) (2009) 'About IFFS', *International Film Festival Summit Website*. On-line. Available HTTP: http://www.filmfestivalsummit.com/aboutus.html (24 September 2012).

Iordanova, Dina (2009) 'The Festival Circuit', in Dina Iordanova and Ragan Rhyne (eds) *Film Festival Yearbook 1: The Festival Circuit*. St. Andrews: St Andrews Film Studies with College Gate Press, 23-38.

Iordanova, Dina and Ragan Rhyne (2009) 'Introduction', in Dina Iordanova and Ragan Rhyne (eds) *Film Festival Yearbook 1: The Festival Circuit*. St. Andrews: St Andrews Film Studies with College Gate Press, 1-5.

Iordanova, Dina and Ragan Rhyne (eds) (2009) *Film Festival Yearbook 1: The Festival Circuit*. St. Andrews: St Andrews Film Studies with College Gate Press.

James, Alison and Leslie Nesselson (2004) '"Grace" Gets Deauville Nod', *Variety*. On-line. Available HTTP: http://www.variety.com/article/ VR1117910311.html (24 September 2012).

Jarman, Claude (2009) Interview by L. Tanner, in Tanner, Lauri Rose (ed.) (2009) *Creating Film Festivals: Everything You Wanted to Know but Didn't Know Who to Ask*. Oakland: Lauri Rose Tanner, 106-113.

Johnson, Brian D. (2000) *Brave Films Wild Nights: 25 Years of Festival Fever*. Toronto: Random House of Canada.

Katz, Daniel and Robert L. Kahn (1978) *The Social Psychology of Organizations*. New York: John Wiley & Sons.

Kaufman, Deborah (2009) Interview by L. Tanner, in Tanner, Lauri Rose (ed.) (2009) *Creating Film Festivals: Everything You Wanted to Know but Didn't Know Who to Ask*. Oakland: Lauri Rose Tanner, 78-84.

Kelly, Brendan (2004a) 'Canucks Clamor for Montréal Alternative', *Variety*. On-line. Available HTTP: http://www.variety.com/article/ VR1117910071.html (24 September 2012).

Kelly, Brendan (2004b) 'Fest Fight Going to Court: Lawsuit Demands $2.1 Million in Damages from Telefilm', *Variety*. On-line. Available HTTP: http://www.variety.com/article/VR1117914870. html?categoryid=22&cs=1 (24 September 2012).

Kelly, Brendan (2007) 'Montreal Festival Bounces Back', *Variety* On-line. Available HTTP: http://www.variety.com/article/VR1117970952. html (24 September 2012).

Kerkinos, Dimitris (2009) 'Programming Balkan Films at the Thessaloniki International Film Festival', in Dina Iordanova and Ragan Rhyne (eds) *Film Festival Yearbook 1: The Festival Circuit*. St. Andrews: St Andrews Film Studies with College Gate Press, 168-175.

Klady, Leonard (1998) 'Chicago International Film Festival (33rd)', in Steve Gaydos (ed.) *The Variety Guide to Film Festivals: The Ultimate Insider's Guide to Film Festivals Around the World*. New York: Berkley Publishing Group, 152-154.

Koehler, Robert (2009) 'Cinephilia and Film Festivals', in Richard Porton (ed.) *Dekalog 3: On Film Festivals*. London: Wallflower Press, 81-97.

Kriedemann, Kevin (2009) 'Durban Film Festival Turns 30', *Variety*. On-line. Available HTTP: http://www.variety.com/article/VR1118006101.html?categoryid=13&cs=1 (24 September 2012).

Langer, Adam (2000) *The Film Festival Guide*. Chicago: Chicago Review Press.

Lazaruk, Ewa (2004) 'Cracow Film Festival, Poland, June 2004', *Norsk Filmklubbforbund*. On-line. Available HTTP: http://ficc.info/IFFS.php?id=1291&t=iffs_reports (24 September 2012).

Lumpkin, Michael (2009) Interview by L. Tanner, in Tanner, Lauri Rose (ed.) (2009) *Creating Film Festivals: Everything You Wanted to Know but Didn't Know Who to Ask*. Oakland: Lauri Rose Tanner, 127-131.

Macdonald, Darryl (1998) 'How to Launch a Community Fest', in Steven Gaydos (ed.) *The Variety Guide to Film Festivals: The Ultimate Insider's Guide to Film Festivals Around the World*. New York: Berkley Publishing Group, 35-44.

Macnab, Geoffrey (2009) 'Zurich Film Festival Stunned by Polanski Arrest', *Screen Daily*. On-line. Available HTTP: http://www.screendaily.com/festivals/other-festivals/festival-news/zurich-film-festival-stunned-by-polanski-arrest/5006129.article (24 September 2012).

Macquarie Dictionary (1997) 'System', *The Macquarie Dictionary*. North Rhyde, NSW: Macquarie Library.

Martin, Adrian (2009) 'Here and Elsewhere (the View from Australia)', in Richard Porton (ed.) *Dekalog 3: On Film Festivals*. London: Wallflower Press, 98-106.

Masters, Charles (2004) 'Fests Play by New Rules', *Backstage.com*. On-
line. Available HTTP: http://www.backstage.com/bso/esearch/
article_display.jsp?vnu_content_id=1000617591 (31 March 2012
– broken URL).

Mayorga, Emilio (2006) 'Madrid Sets Up New Film Festival', *Variety*.
On-line. Available HTTP: http://www.variety.com/article/
VR1117955572.html (24 September 2012).

McCarthy, Todd (1997) 'Introduction', in Peter Bart (ed.) *Cannes: Fifty
Years of Sun, Sex & Celluloid*. New York: Berkley Publishing Group,
11-17.

McCarthy, Todd (1998) 'Santa Barbara International Film Festival (13th)', in
Steven Gaydos (ed.) *The Variety Guide to Film Festivals: The Ultimate
Insider's Guide to Film Festivals Around the World*. New York: Berkley
Publishing Group, 67-8.

McCarthy, Todd (2004) 'Sundance Stepping to an Int'l Rhythm', *Variety*.
On-line. Available HTTP: http://www.variety.com/index.asp?layo
ut=story&articleid=VR1117914097&categoryid=1236&cs=1 (24
September 2012).

Melbourne International Film Festival (MIFF) (2012) 'Submission
Regulations', On-line. Available HTTP: http://miff.com.au/films/
films/film_entry_2012/entry_regulations (24 September 2012).

Meyer, Gary (2009) Interview by L. Tanner, in Tanner, Lauri Rose (ed.)
(2009) *Creating Film Festivals: Everything You Wanted to Know but
Didn't Know Who to Ask*. Oakland: Lauri Rose Tanner, 71-77.

Meyer, John W. and Brian Rowan (1983) 'Institutionalized Organizations:
Formal Structure as Myth and Ceremony', in Meyer, John
W., W. Richard Scott, Brian Rowan and Terrence E. Deal (eds)
Organizational Environments: Ritual and Rationality. Beverly Hills:
Sage Publications, 21-44.

Meyer, John W., W. Richard Scott, Brian Rowan and Terrence E. Deal (1983) *Organizational Environments: Ritual and Rationality*. Beverly Hills: SAGE Publications.

Meza, Ed (2009) 'VW Backs Out of Berlin Sponsorship', *Variety*. On-line. Available HTTP: http:// http://www.variety.com/article/ VR1118003019 (24 September 2012).

Milan Film Festival (2009) 'The Festival is Over – See You in 2010', Personal correspondence with Author. September 22, 2009.

Milofsky, Carl (ed) (1988) *Community Organizations: Studies in Resource Mobilization and Exchange*. New York: Oxford University Press.

Mohr, Ian (2005) 'Rendez-Vous Ready', *Variety*. On-line. Available HTTP: http://www.variety.com/article/VR1117917516.html (24 September 2012).

Möller, Olaf (2009) 'Bagatelle for Kino Otok and i 1000 Occhi', in Richard Porton (ed.) *Dekalog 3: On Film Festivals*. London: Wallflower Press, 143-50.

Parinyaporn Pajee (2009) 'BIFF Downsized, to Focus on Asian Films', *The Nation*. On-line. Available HTTP: http://www.nationmultimedia. com/home/2007/07/01//BIFF-downsized-to-focus-on-Asian-films-30038343.html (24 September 2012).

Parsons, Talcott (1951) *The Social System*. New York: Free Press.

Peranson, Mark (2009) 'First You Get the Power, Then You Get the Money: Two Models of Film Festivals', in Richard Porton (ed.) *Dekalog 3: On Film Festivals*. London: Wallflower Press, 23-37.

Pfeffer, Jeffrey and Gerald R. Salancik (2003) *The External Control of Organizations: A Resource Dependence Perspective*. Stanford: Stanford University Press.

Poirier, Agnes (2003) 'Montreal Festival Deprived of 'A-list' Status', *Screen Daily.com*. On-line. Available HTTP: http://www.screendaily.com/ montreal-festival-deprived-of-a-list-status/4013701.article (24 September 2012).

Porton, Richard (ed.) (2009) *Dekalog 3: On Film Festivals*. London: Wallflower Press.

Porybna, Tereza (ed.) (2009) *Setting up a Human Rights Film Festival*. Prague: People In Need. Online. Available HTTP: http://www. oneworld.cz/2011/userfiles/file/OW-cookbook_web.pdf (24 September 2012).

Pratley, Gerald and Leonard Klady (1998) 'A Short History of International Film Festivals', in Steven Gaydos (ed.) *The Variety Guide to Film Festivals: The Ultimate Insider's Guide to Film Festivals around the World*. New York: Berkley Publishing Group, 1-6.

Queensland Events (2009) 'Events Calendar', *Queensland Events*. On-line. Available HTTP: http://www.qldevents.com.au/events/details. php?eventId=860&r=6&et=1 (26 November 2011 – broken URL).

Queensland Government (2009) 'Population and Housing Fact Sheet', *Queensland Government Department of Infrastructure and Planning*. On-line. Available HTTP: http://www.dip.qld.gov.au/resources/ map/population-housing-factsheets/gold-coast-city-council.pdf (24 September 2012).

Rayns, Tony (2009) Interview by L. Tanner, in Tanner, Lauri Rose (ed.) (2009) *Creating Film Festivals: Everything You Wanted to Know but Didn't Know Who to Ask*. Oakland: Lauri Rose Tanner, 85-93.

Rhyne, Ragan (2009) 'Film Festival Circuits and Stakeholders', in Dina Iordanova and Ragan Rhyne (eds) *Film Festival Yearbook 1: The Festival Circuit*. St. Andrews: St Andrews Film Studies with College Gate Press, 9-22.

Rithdee, Kong (2009) 'The Sad Case of the Bangkok Film Festival', in Richard Porton (ed.) *Dekalog 3: On Film Festivals*. London: Wallflower Press, 122-30.

Robinson, Cathy (2006) Interview with the Chief Executive of the Australian Film Commission (1989-1999); President of the Sydney Film Festival (2000-2005), Interview in Gold Coast, 22 April 2006, by Alex Fischer.

Roddick, Nick (2009) 'Coming to a Server Near You: The Film Festival in the Age of Digital Reproduction', in Dina Iordanova and Ragan Rhyne (eds) *Film Festival Yearbook 1: The Festival Circuit*. St. Andrews: St Andrews Film Studies with College Gate Press, 159-167.

Roelofs, Laura Leigh (2008) 'Open Systems Concepts', *Organizational Change*. On-line. Available HTTP: http://www.soi.org/reading/change/concepts.shtml (24 November 2011 – broken URL).

Rooney, David (1998) 'Venice International Film Festival', in Steven Gaydos (ed.) *The Variety Guide to Film Festivals: The Ultimate Insider's Guide to Film Festivals Around the World*. New York: Berkley Publishing Group, 120-22.

Rosenbaum, Jonathan (2009) 'Some Festivals I've Known: A Few Rambling Recollections', in Richard Porton (ed.) *Dekalog 3: On Film Festivals*. London: Wallflower Press, 151-65.

Rosenthal, Henry (2009) Interview by L. Tanner, in Tanner, Lauri Rose (ed.) (2009) *Creating Film Festivals: Everything You Wanted to Know but Didn't Know Who to Ask*. Oakland: Lauri Rose Tanner, 33-36.

Screen Producers Association of Australia (2009) 'About SPAA', *Screen Producers Association of Australia*. On-line. Available HTTP: http://www.spaa.org.au/displaycommon.cfm?an=3 (24 September 2012).

SECOR Consulting (2004) *Analysis of Canada's Major Film Festivals*. Montréal: SECOR Consulting. On-line. Available HTTP: http://www.telefilm.ca/upload/fonds_prog/secor-report.pdf (24 September 2012).

Selwyn, Michael (2006) Interview with the Managing Director of Paramount Pictures Australia (formally United International Pictures (UIP)). Interview in Gold Coast, 24 August 2006, by Alex Fischer.

Silva, Gail (2009) Interview by L. Tanner, in Tanner, Lauri Rose (ed.) (2009) *Creating Film Festivals: Everything You Wanted to Know but Didn't Know Who to Ask*. Oakland: Lauri Rose Tanner, 68-70.

Slocum, J. David (2009) 'Film and/as Culture: The Use of Cultural Discourses at Two African Film Festivals', in Dina Iordanova and Ragan Rhyne (eds) *Film Festival Yearbook 1: The Festival Circuit*. St. Andrews: St Andrews Film Studies with College Gate Press, 136-52.

Smith, Lory (1999) *Party In A Box: The Story of the Sundance Film Festival*. Salt Lake City: Gibbs Smith.

Softpedia (2006) 'Robert De Niro's Film Festival in New York Has Begun!', *Softpedia.com*. On-line. Available HTTP: http://news.softpedia.com/news/Robert-De-Niro-039-s-film-festival-in-New-York-has-begun-22114.shtml (24 September 2012).

Starnes, Becky J. (2000) 'Achieving Competitive Advantage Through the Application of Open Systems Theory and the Development of Strategic Alliances: A Guide for Managers of Nonprofit Organizations', *Journal of Nonprofit & Public Sector Marketing*, 8, 2, 15-27.

Stolberg, Shael (ed.) (2000) *International Film Festival Guide*. Toronto: Festival Products.

Stone, Marla (1999) 'Challenging Cultural Categories: The Transformation of the Venice Biennale Under Fascism', *Journal of Modern Italian Studies*, 4, 2, 184- 208.

Stone, Marla (2002) 'The Last Film Festival: The Venice Biennale Goes to War', in Jacqueline Reich and Piero Garofalo (eds) *Re-viewing Fascism: Italian Cinema 1922-1943*. Indiana University Press, 293-314.

Stringer, Julian (2001) 'Global Cities and the International Film Festival Economy', in Mark Shiel and Tony Fitzmaurice (eds) *Cinema and the City: Film and Urban Societies in a Global Context*. London: Blackwell Publishers, 134-44.

Alex Fischer

Stringer, Julian (ed.) (2003) *Movie Blockbusters*. London: Routledge.

Svenson, Michelle (2001) 'How to Start Your Own Film Festival', *Koreanfilm.org*. On-line. Available HTTP: http://www.koreanfilm. org/startfest.html (24 September 2012).

Tanner, Lauri Rose (ed.) (2009) *Creating Film Festivals: Everything You Wanted to Know But Didn't Know Who to Ask*. Oakland: Lauri Rose Tanner.

Telefilm (2007) 'Festivals in Montréal', *Telefilm Canada*. On-line. Available HTTP: http://www2.telefilm.gc.ca/07/782. asp?Print=True&Lang=EN (15 October 2011 – broken URL).

Telefilm (2010) 'Canada on The Festival Circuit Abroad', *Telefilm Canada*. On-line. Available HTTP: http://www.telefilm.gc.ca/en/ festivals-and-markets/canada-on-the-festival-circuit-abroad (24 September 2012).

Teo, Stephen (2009) 'Asian Film Festivals and Their Diminishing Glitter Domes: An Appraisal of PIFF, SIFF and HKIFF', in Richard Porton (ed.) *Dekalog 3: On Film Festivals*. London: Wallflower Press, 109-21.

The Filmlot (2006) 'The Filmlot Fest Blog: Resources for New and Independent Filmmakers', *thefilmlot.com*. On-line. Available HTTP: http://thefilmlot.com/ (23 November 2011).

Tizard, Will (2005) 'Karlovy Vary Adds Glitz', *Variety*. On-line. Available HTTP: http://www.variety.com/article/VR1117925419.html (24 September 2012).

Tropfest (2008) 'Signature Item', *Tropfest.com*. On-line. Available HTTP: http://www.tropfest.com/au/SignatureItem.aspx (31 March 2012 – broken URL).

Turan, Kenneth (2002) *Sundance to Sarajevo: Film Festivals and the World They Make*. Berkeley and Los Angeles: University of California Press.

Vancouver International Film Center (2008) 'VIFF Mandate and Acknowledgements', *Vancouver International Film Center*. On-line. Available HTTP: http://www.viff.org/theatre/about/ (25 November 2011).

Vivarelli, Nick (2004) 'H'wood Signs on Lido', *Variety*. On-line. Available HTTP: http://www.variety.com/article/VR1117903961.html (24 September 2012).

Vourlias, Christopher (2012) 'Sierra Leone Presents First Film Fest', *Variety*. On-line. Available HTTP: http://www.variety.com/article/ VR1118052264 (24 September 2012).

Wall, James M. (2009) 'Ron Holloway Finds "Political Movies" at the 2009 Berlin Festival', *Wallwritings.wordpress.com* On-line. Available HTTP: http://wallwritings.wordpress.com/2009/03/20/ron-holloway-finds-political-movies-at-the-2009-berlin-festival/ (24 September 2012).

Webber, Pauline (2005) *History of the Sydney Film Festival*. Unpublished Masters Thesis, University of Technology Sydney, Australia.

Yee, Jim (2009) Interview by L. Tanner, in Tanner, Lauri Rose (ed.) (2009) *Creating Film Festivals: Everything You Wanted to Know but Didn't Know Who to Ask*. Oakland: Lauri Rose Tanner, 141-145.

Filmography

$9.99 (Tatia Rosenthal, Israel, Australia 2009)

Babe (Chris Noonan, Australia, U.S., 1995)

Braveheart (Mel Gibson, U.S., 1995)

Dare mo shiranai / Nobody Knows (Hirokazu Kore-Eda, Japan, 2004)

Free Enterprise (Robert Meyer Burnett, U.S., 1998)

Ghost Town (David Keopp, U.S., 2008)

Highwater (Dana Brown, U.S., 2009)

Hustle & Flow (Craig Brewer, U.S., 2005)

Looking for Eric (Ken Loach, UK, France, Italy, Belgium, Spain, 2009)

Salute (Matt Norman, Australia, U.S., 2008)

Sex, Lies, and Videotape (Steven Soderbergh, U.S., 1989)

Shark Tale (Bibo Bergeron, Vicky Jenson, Rob Letterman, U.S., 2004)

Step into Liquid (Dana Brown, U.S., 2003)

The Libertine (Laurence Dunmore, U.S., 2004)

The Ruins (Carter Smith, U.S., 2008)

Tobira no muko / Left Handed (Laurence Thrush, Japan, 2008)

List of Film Festivals

48-Hour Film Project

Angelus Awards Student Film Festival

Art Film Festival

Atlantic Film Festival

Aurora Asian Film Festival

Bangkok International Film Festival

Bergen International Film Festival

Berlin International Film Festival

Brainwash Movie Festival

Brisbane International Film Festival

Busan International Film Festival

Brussels International Fantastic Film Festival

Cairo International Film Festival

Cannes International Film Festival

Chicago International Film Festival

Charged 60-second Film Festival

CIM Madrid International Film Festival

Cine Acción Cine Latino

Cinequest San Jose Film Festival

Cochin International Film Festival

Cracow Film Festival

Cucalorus Film Festival

Alex Fischer

Dances with Films

Deauville American Films Festival

Denver International Film Festival

Donostia-San Sebastian Horror and Fantasy Film Festival

Durban Film Festival

Edinburgh International Film Festival

Edmonds International Film Festival

Experimental Film Festival

Fantasporto: Oporto International Film Festival

Fantasia International Film Festival

Festival du Court Métrage en Plein Air de Grenoble

Film Arts Festival

Flanders International Film Festival

Flickerfest

Freaky Film Festival

Freedom Film Festival

Gold Coast Film Fantastic

Gothenburg Film Festival

Hi Mom! Film Festival

Hof International Film Festival

Hong Kong International Film Festival

Human Rights Watch International Film Festival

International Children's Film Festival LUCAS

International Film Cinematographers' Film Festival "Manaki Brothers"

International Film Festival Arsenals

International Film Festival Rotterdam

International Young Audience Film Festival Ale Kino

Karlovy Vary International Film Festival

Kino Otok (Cinema Island)

Kinotavr Film Festival

Leeds International Film Festival

Leofest

Locarno International Film Festival

Los Angeles Gay and Lesbian Film Festival

Los Angeles Latino International Film Festival

London Film Festival

Manifestazione Cinematografica Italo-Germanica

Max Ophüls Preis Film Festival

Melbourne International Film Festival

Milano Film Festival

Mill Valley Film Festival

Minghella Film Festival

Moscow International Film Festival

New York Expo of Short Film and Video

New York Film Festival

New York Lesbian and Gay Film Festival

Northwest Film & Video Festival

Noosa Film Festival

Palm Springs International Film Festival

Palm Springs Festival of Short Films

Prague International Film Festival

Puchon International Fantastic Film Festival

Roger Ebert's Overlooked Film Festival

Royal Anthropological Institute's International Festival of Ethnographic Film

San Francisco International Asian American Film Festival

San Francisco International Film Festival

San Francisco Jewish Film Festival

San Francisco International Lesbian and Gay Film Festival (Frameline)

San Sébastian International Film Festival

Sierra Leone International Film Festival

Singapore International Film Festival

Skip City International D-Cinema Festival

Small Pictures International Film Festival

South by Southwest

Stockholm International Film Festival

Sydney Film Festival

Seattle International Film Festival

Slamdance Film Festival

Sundance

Tallinn Black Night Film Festival

Taos Talking Pictures Film Festival

Tech TV's Cam Film Festival

Telluride Film Festival

The New York Lesbian and Gay Experimental Film Festival

Thessaloniki International Film Festival

Tokyo International Film Festival

Toronto International Film Festival

Tribeca Film Festival

Tropfest

Tudela First Film Festival

Vancouver International Film Festival

Venice Arts Biennale

Venice International Film Festival

Videotivoli Video Festival for Children and Young People

Whistler Film Festival

Women and Film International Festival

Women in the Director's Chair Film Festival

Women's Film Festival

World Film Festival

World's Worst Movies Festival

Zanzibar International Film Festival

Zurich Film Festival

Films Need Festivals, Festivals Need Films

Series Editor: Dina Iordanova

Advisory Board: Chris Berry (London), Marc Cousins (Edinburgh), Marijke de Valck (Amsterdam), James English (Philadelphia), Jean-Michel Frodon (Paris), Lee Yong-kwan (Busan), Richard Porton (New York).

Films Need Festivals: All films seek exposure and, for many films, festivals are among the few available platforms that give such exposure. Yet, the festival circuit is a platform that is insufficiently explored and remains poorly understood.

Festivals Need Films: Having come into existence once, film festivals have an insatiable need for new content. Festivals depend on films for their own survival, threading the fine line between opulence and obscurity.

Work published in this series will improve the understanding of the way film travels through the festival circuit. It seeks to highlight and untangle the dialectics of the two. Conceptually, the project is based on notions of transnationalism and dialogism. It will pay attention to peripheral yet significant phenomena and will bring about new insights by breaking down the concept of a single festival circuit into many smaller self-contained yet interlocking clusters.

The series seeks to capture the dynamics of global film festivals. It will be comprehensive in its geographical coverage, with examples not only from the West but also stretching as far as Latin America and Africa and acknowledging the key importance of Asia. It will seek to analyze the reasons for the proliferation of film festivals in some cultural contexts as opposed to their restrained advancement in others. It will seek to show the range of stakeholders and forces that shape the film festival in relationship to tourism, cultural diplomacy or various activist causes. It will explore management and political aspects and the so-called economies of prestige. Last but not least, it will explore the relentless invasion of the digital forms of distribution and how they change the game.

Be in touch if you would like to discuss your proposal.

St Andrews Film Studies
St Andrews, Scotland
www.stafs.org

Film Festival Yearbook 1:
THE FESTIVAL CIRCUIT

Edited by Dina Iordanova with Ragan Rhyne

The annual series of *Film Festival Yearbooks* seeks to redress a gap in current scholarship, theorising the nature and functioning of film festivals and the festival circuit and providing case studies and resources to facilitate further research into this important and burgeoning field.

The first volume, *The Festival Circuit*, features articles related to the global proliferation of film festivals and focuses on the dynamics of the film festival circuit, including the roles played by individual festivals as nodes on this complex network and the cultural policies that shape its channels of film exhibition and distribution.

St Andrews Film Studies with College Gate Press, 2009
Paperback ISBN: 978-1-906678-04-3
Price: £17.99

Available from **www.stafs.org**
and all good book suppliers.

"The *Film Festival Yearbook* project represents a unique opportunity to study the multi-faceted phenomenon of film festivals. It focuses on both global networks and local practices and sheds new light on the artistic, economic and political issues that are currently reshaping the global cultural field. Bringing together academics and practitioners from an impressively wide range of professional and national origins, it embraces both empirical and theoretical analysis. In so doing it provides striking new insights into a hugely significant cultural phenomenon."

Jean Michel Frodon (film critic, Paris, France)

"The study of film festivals has thus far been limited to case studies of individual festivals, often comprising only organisers' reports. It is not the aim of [the *Film Festival Yearbook*] project to discredit this methodology...it is instead to provide a more comprehensive approach to festival studies, one where empirical data, and organizational narratives come together with an attempt to theorise the very idea of film festivals...The series is a welcome addition to the discipline."

Kuhu Tanvir, 'Book Review: Film Festival Yearbook 1: The Festival Circuit', *Wide Screen*, 1:2, June 2010

Film Festival Yearbook 2: FILM FESTIVALS AND IMAGINED COMMUNITIES

Edited by Dina Iordanova with Ruby Cheung

The second volume in the *Film Festival Yearbook* series brings together essays about festivals that use international cinema to mediate the creation of transnational 'imagined communities'. There are texts about the cultural policies and funding models linked to these festivals, as well as analysis of programming practices linked to these often highly politicised events. The case studies discuss diaspora-linked festivals that take place in Vienna, San Francisco, San Sebastian, Havana, Bradford, Sahara, South Korea and London and that feature cinema from places as diverse as Nepal and Kurdistan, Africa and Latin America.

St Andrews Film Studies, 2010
Paperback ISBN: 978-0-9563730-1-4
Price: £17.99 (paperback), 286 pages

"The very ambitious aspiration of the Film Festival Yearbook is, quite literally, to define a new area of film study."

Jonathan Rosenbaum (film critic and author)

"Most publications on film festivals so far have been anecdotal case studies, brief journalistic reports and anniversary books. St Andrews' FFY series is the first major academic book series devoted to the phenomenon of film festivals. The editors treat the subject as an emerging discipline within film and media studies that has taken a clear departure from both fields because film festival study is multiple and interdisciplinary in nature...The editorial vision declared in the FFY series is to deveop a systematic approach to explain, theorize and historicize film festivals in order to understand the subject in greater detail and with more intellectual rigour... [The] books make vital contributions to the burgeoning area of film festival studies."

Ming-Yeh T. Rawnsley, 'Film Festival Yearbok 1: The Festival Circuit/ Film Festival Yearbook 2: Film Festivals and Imagined Communities', *Transnational Cinemas*, 2:1. 2011, pp.120-122.

Available from **www.stafs.org** and all good book suppliers.

Film Festival Yearbook 3:
FILM FESTIVALS AND EAST ASIA

Edited by Dina Iordanova with Ruby Cheung

The most exciting developments in world cinema over the past two decades have been linked to East Asian countries such as China, Japan and South Korea. Films made in East Asia triumph at festivals around the globe. Booming film markets are attached to the most important film festivals in Hong Kong, Pusan, Tokyo and Shanghai. The West is only just beginning to wake up to the importance of these film festivals to global film distribution.

In the latest volume of the *Film Festivals Yearbook*, scholars from the University of St. Andrews and beyond chart these cutting-edge developments in global film. And by opening up debates on the worldwide network of film festivals, they lay the necessary groundwork for a greater understanding of global film circulation.

St Andrews Film Studies, 2011
ISBN: 978-0-9563730-3-8 (paperback) 978-0-9563730-4-5 (hardback)
PRICE: £19.99 (paperback); £50.00 (hardback), 292 pages

East Asia and Film Festivals: Transnational Clusters for Creativity and Commerce (Dina Iordanova)

Part I: Contexts
Asian Film Festivals, Translation and the International Film Festival Short Circuit (Abé Mark Nornes)
East Asian Film Festivals: Film Markets (Ruby Cheung)
Japan 1951-1970: National Cinema as Cultural Currency (Julian Stringer)
News for Whom? Critical Coverage of the 10th Jeonju International Film Festival (Adrian Martin)
Washington, Pusan, Rotterdam, Udine and Back: Programming East Asian Films for American Audiences (Tom Vick)

Part II: Case Studies
Bulldozers, Bibles and Very Sharp Knives: The Chinese Independent Documentary Scene (Abé Mark Nornes)
Comrades and Citizens: Gay and Lesbian Film Festivals in China (Ragan Rhyne)
Programming Southeast Asia at the Singapore International Film Festival (Felicia Chan and Dave Chua)
Taipei Film Festival: Creation of a Global City (Yun-hua Chen)
Tourism and the Landscape of Thai Film Festivals (Adam Knee and Kong Rithdee)
North Korea's Pyongyang International Film Festival (James Bell)
Between Europe and Asia? A Chronicle of the 'Eurasia' International Film Festival (Kazakhstan) (Birgit Beumers)

Part III: Resources
The Resources: Necessary Groundwork (Dina Iordanova)
Interviews
Tables
Location Map

"This new anthology captures the enthusiasm for East Asian cinema felt by film lovers and film professionals the world over."

Chris Fujiwara (editor of *Undercurrent*)

"A vital contribution to both Asian Film Studies and Film Festival Studies."

Chris Berry (Goldsmiths University of London)

"This valuable book…gathers sharp and thought-provoking analyses from a variety of viewpoints…It offers useful groundwork for a better understanding of why film festivals in general, and Asian film festivals in particular, matter to anyone interested in cinema as an internationally dispersed and engaged art form."

Shelly Kraicer, 'Film Festival Yearbook 3: Film Festivals and East Asia', *Cineaste*, 37:2, Spring 2012, pp.65-66.

Available from **www.stafs.org**
and all good book suppliers.

Film Festival Yearbook 4:
FILM FESTIVALS AND ACTIVISM

Edited by Dina Iordanova and Leshu Torchin

Film festivals not only build markets and audiences, they also provide platforms for those advocating for change, and in recent years have been playing an increasing role in social justice movements and campaigns. Bringing together the perspectives of scholars, programmers, filmmakers and activists, *Film Festivals and Activism* provides essential insight into the nature, function and practice of activist film festivals. With interviews, conceptual overviews, case studies, histories, bibliographies, and tables of festivals around the world, this volume offers an invaluable resource for scholars and practitioners alike.

St Andrews Film Studies, 2012
ISBN: 978-0-9563730-5-2 (paperback); 978-0-9563730-6-9 (hardback)
PRICE: £19.99 (paperback); £50.00 (hardback), 317 pages

Part 1: Contexts
Networked for Advocacy: Film Festivals and Activism
Film Festivals and Dissent: Can Film Change the World?
Human Rights Film Festivals: Global/Local Networks for Social Justice and Advocacy
On the Development of Queer Film Festivals and Their Media Activism
Towards an Indigenous Film Festival Circuit
Permutations of the Species: Independent Disability Cinema and the Critique of National Normativity
Traffic Jam Revisited: Film Festivals, Activism and Human Trafficking

Part 2: Case Studies
Film Festivals as a Human Rights Awareness Building Tool: Experiences of the Prague One World Festival
A Cinematic Refuge in the Desert. Festival Internacional de Cine del Sahara
'Tell Our Story to the World': The Meaning of Success for A Massacre Foretold – A Filmmaker Reflects
Voices from the Waters. International Travelling Film Festival on Water
Mediterranean Encounters in Rabat: Rencontres méditerranéennes cinéma et droits de l'Homme
Human Rights Film Festivals as an Emerging Model of Human Rights Education: The Human Rights Arts and Film Festival (HRAFF), Australia
Humanist and Poetic Activism: The Robert Flaherty Film Seminar in the 1950s

Part 3: Resources
The Resources: Groundwork Continued
From Local to Global: The Growing Pains of the Human Rights Watch International Film Festival: An Interview with Bruni Burres, Festival Director (1991-2008)
Combining the Foreign with the Familiar: An Interview with Jasmina Bojic, Founder and Director of the United Nations Association Film Festival
Hot Docs: A Prescription for Reality: An Interview with Sean Farnel, Former Director of Programming at Hot Docs Canadian International Documentary Festival
Just Vision and the Uses of a Festival Circuit: An Interview with Ronit Avni, Executive Director of Just Vision
'Connect Me with Activism and Film Practice, Not Activism and Film Festivals!': An Interview with Želimir Žilnik, Filmmaker
How to Leverage a Film Festival: An Interview with Judith Helfand, Filmmaker and Co-founder of Chicken & Egg Pictures and Working Films
The Human Touch: A Review of the One World Human Rights Film Festival Handbook

"*Film Festivals and Activism* provides an excellent overview of the field of human rights and other activist film festivals. It combines field-level synthesis by academics with expertise in both film festivals and human rights activism and employs a range of perspectives from key protagonists working in both established and new festival settings."

Sam Gregory (Programme Director, Witness, New York, USA)

"*Film Festivals and Activism* constitutes a profound acknowledgement of the work carried out by film festivals and contains a wealth of useful information about the ideas behind them. It manages to convey the great diversity of the international film circuit, featuring contributions that range from the traditionally academic to the engagingly essayistic. Film Festivals and Activism clearly demonstrates the need for this kind of publication in academic film studies and, most importantly, provides a valuable resource for anyone planning or working with international film festivals.

Bjørn Sørenssen (Professor of Film and Media, Trondheim, Norway)

Available from **www.stafs.org** and all good book suppliers.

Coming Soon to a Festival Near You: Programming Film Festivals

Edited by Jeffrey Ruoff

Film festivals are live, communal affairs. Screenings, events, interviews, concerts etc. are part of every festival. This book demonstrates that the best programming has an inner logic, or narrative structure, that finds audiences for films and films for audiences. This is the first scholarly anthology to examine the fundamental role of programming in film festival culture. Featuring contributions from an impressive range of scholars and festival programmers, the book makes a valuable contribution to the growing field of film festival scholarship.

Publisher: St Andrews Film Studies
Paperback ISBN: 978-1-908437-02-0
Price: £19.99

REVIEWS

"This is an outstanding anthology of work on film-festival programming. Combining theoretical and historical overviews with detailed studies of individual festivals and personal testimonies from experts long associated with film festivals, the book makes a thorough, wide-ranging and insightful effort at covering a field that has been significantly neglected in scholarship. As the first book to make film-festival programming its main focus, the book should be considered an essential contribution to the growing body of published work on film festivals." **Chris Fujiwara** (Artistic Director, Edinburgh International Film Festival)

"By focusing specifically on programming strategies, *Coming Soon to a Theatre near You* gives a new twist to the frequently discussed topic of film festivals as 'alternative distribution networks'. The book makes a distinctive contribution to the field by fusing certain preoccupations in the burgeoning area of festival studies with the intricacies of programming." **Richard Porton** (*Cineaste*)

"Jeffrey Ruoff has tracked down film festival insiders as well as key researchers in the emergent field of film-festival studies. The combination makes for a valuable synergistic anthology that lays bare the inner workings of a world too often trivialized or deified by those who don't realize what transpires 'behind the curtain.' This important collection raises the bar on festival writing, interrogates questions of taste and marketing, and offers a model for the next stage of study." **B. Ruby Rich** (Professor of Film and Digital Media, University of California, Santa Cruz)

Available from **www.stafs.org**
and all good book suppliers.

Lightning Source UK Ltd.
Milton Keynes UK
UKOW05f1914030414

229339UK00001B/19/P

9 780956 373083